GEORGIA ON MY MIND:
AN ANTHOLOGY OF CONTEMPORARY WRITERS

RENAISSANCE PRESS

MACON, GEORGIA—1983

Library of Congress Catalog Card Number 83-063267
ISBN 0-914707-00-0

Printed at Braun-Brumfield, Inc.
Ann Arbor, Michigan

CONTENTS

Foreword

GEORGIA ON MY MIND: AN ANTHOLOGY OF CON-TEMPORARY WRITERS is the initial publication of the newly founded RENAISSANCE PRESS, whose purpose is to bring to the surface the talent of gifted writers in our midst.

The volume here offered presents a wide assortment of creative materials, most of which come from native Georgians. Chosen from among scores of responses are over seventy poems, seventeen short stories, two essays, a play, a parable, a riddle, a fable, and other contributions difficult to classify. From Georgia, about Georgia, written while in Georgia, yes; but also represented are Sicily, Canada, Russia, Sodom and Gomorrah, and ancient Rome, not to mention Texas, Kansas, South Dakota, Connecticut and other faraway places. Joys, thoughts on death, reckless abandon, slapstick, heartbreak, childlike awe, courage and honor—all are written in these pages. As Dante found himself expressing gratitude to Brunetto for teaching him one aspect of immortality, so may it be that readers of these words will be encouraged and moved toward thanksgiving by their discovery of these creations drawn from the human spirit.

Critics no doubt will find things to disparage: new twists that defy tradition, conventional styles that suggest the "good old days," a bit of raw profanity—even blasphemings—always unacceptable in certain quarters, high affirmations of faith, objective descriptions that appear too stark residing alongside personal catchings of emanations arising from the nearby and from the beyond. Not all will agree on the decision to list only the names of authors, without further identification; but this reflects a strong conviction that the merits of any accomplishment must be evaluated apart from the previous reputation of the writer. Some, appearing in this volume, have published much; others, not at all. A few are already world-famous; a greater number, barely known in their home country. The variety is astonishing; indeed, it is a Duke's mixture. Yet affirmed in these pages of "red clay and granite" is a vision which excludes neither mystery nor manners, nor the confidence that what the heart sees goes beyond that which meets the eye.

Robert Fox, General Editor
RENAISSANCE PRESS

Macon
November, 1983

Acknowledgments

The editors of RENAISSANCE PRESS happily and gratefully acknowledge the following sources:

Mr. Robert Fitzgerald for permission to use the poem, *The First Book*, by Flannery O'Connor; Mr. Gerald Becham, former curator of the Flannery O'Connor Room, Ina Dillard Russell Library, Georgia College.

Mr. Patrick D. Morrow, SOUTHERN HUMANITIES REVIEW, for permission to use the two stories by Andrew Borders, *Meat of the Dead* and *Ritual*.

Mr. Stanley W. Lindberg, THE GEORGIA REVIEW, for permission to use the essay by F. N. Boney, *The Redneck* (Fall, 1971).

Mr. Jim Leeson of Franklin, Tennessee, for permission to use the historical report of the Reverend Will D. Campbell, *The Death of Willie Gene Carreker*, which appeared in *Race Relations Reporter*, 1974.

Ms. Ginny Herren, *The Dulcimer*, Mercer University for permission to use the story, *Jesus Saves! Jesus Saves!*, by Deborah W. Burkhalter.

We are grateful to Mr. Bruce Hafley, the well-known artist living in Atlanta, for the creation of the dogwood symbol of RENAISSANCE PRESS.

The fiction selections in this anthology are not intended to reflect any real persons or places.

FLANNERY O'CONNOR

The First Book

(unedited)

When man was just a caveman,
In the prehistoric age,
His mind began to wander,
And his bean began to rage.
To think that he had all these years
Been lonesome, dumb and tough,
Without a spot of culture
To make him not so rough.
He took his brain within his hands
And pressed it hard and tight,
Until within his feeble mind,
There shone a spark of light.
Thus inspiration came to man,
And he without delay
Wrote down the words she told him to
On slides of stone and clay.
And when the masterpiece was done
He called his friends to look,
They asked him what he named the thing
He said with ease, "a book."
Thus the ancestor of books was born,
On slides of stone and clay.
How far removed was that old book
From those we have today?
And since we have the chance to read
Let's take it while we can,
How far removed are we today,
From prehistoric man?

Mary Flannery O'Connor
10th Grade, Peabody School
Milledgeville, Georgia

1

DAN METTS, JR.

The Burning Bush

God is love
Love is not God
God is God
God is
IS
IS   IS
IS   IS   IS
IS   IS
IS

God is mighty
Mighty is not God
God is God
God is
IS
IS   IS
IS   IS   IS
IS   IS
IS

God is good
Good is not God
God is God
God is
IS
IS   IS
IS   IS   IS
IS   IS
IS

God is just
Just is not God
God is God
God is
IS
IS   IS
IS   IS   IS
IS   IS
IS

3

The Abba

Cinder-lipped comes the prophet, crater-eyed, and
   wild
From the wilderness comes the Abba, bewildered,
   like a child.
He speaks of demons and a glory that sears the
   heart and mind.
He tells of holy visions seen only by the blind,
While we tend the ordered matrix of this pleasant,
   shady grove,
And wonder, "In that desert do other madmen
   rove?"

Job

I always envied Job;
   crouching alone
He clutched his rotted
   flesh to eggshell bone
While pious fellows
   ringed him round
Searching for spoors
   of God upon the ground,
or, cowering in the cruel
   Sun's shine
They patterned shades
   to give the light design.
Not Job. Impatient, looking
   toward the sky
In anger and in agony he
   cried out, "Why?"

The I AM from the
whirlwind did not
   answer him,
but shone forth
with a glory that
made the question
   dim.
I always envied Job.
Pray for us, Job.

Via Negativa

In a darkness shading darkness,
In a silence echoing silence,
In nothing closed in nothing,
   i-am-that-i-am reaches for
I-AM-THAT-I-AM.
In the reaching darkness is light,
Silence is music,
Nothing is not.

A Parable

A man was going down from Jerusalem to Jericho, and he fell among robbers, who stripped him and beat him, and departed, leaving him half dead. Now by chance a priest was going down that road, and when the man saw him, he called out, "My rights have been violated. I have been robbed and beaten. Now I have a right to medical treatment." But the priest passed by on the other side of the street. Presently a Levite came by and the same thing happened. Later when a Samaritan came by, he stopped. "You don't have any right to any medical treatment," said the Samaritan. "The Traveller's Emergency Medical Treatment Bill is still in committee and won't be up for a vote until August."

"I don't mean that kind of right," said the man. "I mean a human right."

"I don't know about any human rights," said the Samaritan. "Who gave them to you? And what about my rights? Don't I have a right to go down this road without having to make a detour around you? You really look repulsive. You ought to be arrested for blocking traffic."

"God gave me the right not to be robbed and to get medical treatment," said the man. "Dammit, don't just stand there, get me my rights."

"God did no such thing," said the Samaritan. "If he had, I'd have heard about it. And besides, if he did, where was he when you got robbed?"

"I guess he was busy," said the man. "Or maybe he forgot."

At that moment the man was racked by a spasm of pain.

"Ooooh—" he cried. "Brother, for the Love of God! Help me!"

And the Samaritan had compassion, and went to him and bound up his wounds, pouring on oil and wine; then he set him on his own beast and brought him to an inn, and took care of him. And the next day he took out two denarii saying, "Take care of him; and whatever more you spend, I will repay you when I come back."

"In this world," said the man who had been robbed, "a man has to learn to stick up for his rights."

ANDREW BORDERS

Ritual

Charlie, my twelve-year-old brother, is counting cars. I am standing beside him, his shoulder just above my elbow, viewing a lighted arc of night highway from a darkened, second-story room. The highway passes in front of our family's grocery; the grocery is downstairs and we live here, on the second story. Between our building and the highway is a grayish-white—gray here, white there, according to the light—graveled parking lot maybe thirty feet from storefront to highway, and when automobiles turn into this area we can hear the gravel crunch beneath their rubber tires and see a little dust rise through the light and disappear into the darkness above us. Charlie is counting cars to determine how many pass our grocery and how many stop. These are presently the statistics of our lives.

Charlie says, "Thirty-six," as a drab green, almost black because of the night, Chevrolet passes, oblivious to being ceremoniously counted, etched on a yellow pad by a small hand that holds a pencil and writes as if it is digging with a stick into the earth. Charlie smells faintly of fish. His voice is matter-of-factly inflected with a businessman's solemnity for detail, but his eyes, quick to sight me then look away, are somehow childishly apprehensive like the child who, on a merry-go-round, circles in front of his parents and quickly, fearfully searches for them only to look away at their presence. I sense there is courage in what Charlie is doing. He is a soldier, I know, clinging.

"It's ten to nine," I say and then contribute, "Ten more minutes."

At nine p.m. Charlie will discontinue counting cars and take his totals downstairs to our father who is anxious to know the count between eight and nine o'clock this Wednesday night. Our father is charting traffic flow, a technique utilized by chain supermarkets to decipher the course of consumer selection and predict the paths of humans with money to spend. By imitating such big-business mechanics, our father, a dreamer of unbounded and sudden prosperity, is convinced that our small store will overnight become a Wall Street wonder. This is not the first venture we have accompanied him, but this is the first we, especially Charlie, have been included in the ritual of success or failure.

9

We have owned the grocery a year, since I was in the eleventh grade. It's as long as we've lived in one place.

"How much time?" Charlie asks even though I've just told him, but I don't answer and he doesn't seem to notice. He continues watching and counting intently as if scouting enemy territory, reconnoitering troop movements. His uniform is fashioned by the reflection of the tri-colored neon sign hanging from the front of the building just outside the window from which we stand watch. The blinking sign illuminates his visage, green, purple, red; an aureole encircles his close-cropped head, his Easter-egg head. As the large sign blinks through the second-story window, Charlie is instantaneously emblazoned, multicolored. He is beautiful.

"How much time?" he asks. His teeth are magically purple.

"Less than ten minutes." I wait for the sign to be illuminated again so I can see my watch. Then, "About seven."

He adds quickly, "I'm up to forty-three."

"The old man," I point out, "is counting on every twelfth car stopping. That's. . . ."

"Don't tell me what I know. I came up with that figure."

"The old man said it was his."

Charlie studies my face in the light, dark, light. In the light he speaks, his voice incredulous, "Who the hell are you going to believe?"

I sit and tilt backward in the slat-back chair beside the window as Charlie looks away disgustedly. He focuses again on the highway, and I study his Easter-egg head, watch his temples pound, and wonder if he's Napoleon, or perhaps Hamlet in a rubescent, green-charged doublet peering intently from the Elsinore parapet. But no, though his courage is sufficient, he is a child, a child that is more Jack waiting at the beanstalk. In my mind I hear, "Fe fi fo fum, I smell. . . ."

"I got caught cheating today," Charlie suddenly confesses, not looking up from his yellow pad, guiltless in his tone, perfunctory in his utterance.

"You tell mother?"

"Hell no!"

I should've known better than ask, but I do not leave it. I want to understand something. I want Charlie to teach me.

10

"Are you going to tell her?" Again, it's rhetorical, but I am jealous of Charlie—not because of our mother, but because Charlie is not intimidated by authority. I must know the secret of his intrepid nonchalance. I already understand there is a discrepancy in our motivations for the success of this grocery; I want it for security, Charlie wants it to use as a weapon for his own survival. No, he is not Hamlet; he is Jack.

He counts a Buick. "Maybe I'll tell her tomorrow," he says which, for Charlie means "I will never tell her."

I need to see his fear. "You'll be kicked out sooner or later," I say. "They'll call her up to the school."

"Naw, they're giving licks now. You get ten for cheating. No sweat." (Men would follow him. Maybe he's Napoleon.) "No way in hell are they going to scare me with licks."

"What's the time?"

It's five past nine, but I tell him it's nine, and he flops into the opposite slat-back chair to total his numbers.

I watch him a minute, then say, "Your birthday's next month."

"So what?"

"So you'll be thirteen. Start your sex life."

He looks at me suspiciously, his eyes glisten when the sign illuminates the window, and I think I see a culpable mask descend upon his slightly smiling face.

"What makes you think I haven't already?" he asks.

"Haven't what?"

"Haven't you know."

"Sex?"

"Yeah, maybe I have."

"What's it like?" I ask.

"Well, I know it's better than the watermelon thing you and Buddy Ray told me back in Atlanta. I tried that," he continues, pointing his pencil at me. "I cut a hole in it just like you said, but a girl's a lot better."

"What girl?"

"I can't tell you."

"That means there isn't one."

He tries to put the pencil to the pad, to write, but he can't. The pencil points back at me.

11

"Jan Funderburk."

"You're lying."

"I don't lie about my sex life," his twelve-year-old voice says menacingly.

"Then what did you do?"

"Felt it."

"That's all?"

"Naw, of course not."

"Well what else?"

"Look," he says, brandishing the pencil toward me like a sword, "if you don't know, then you've never done it yourself." He seems satisfied with his parry, slumps a bit forward, and scribbles, unvanquished, on his yellow pad.

To see better he pushes his chair a foot or two backwards away from the spectacular blinking of the sign and into an almost hazy area between the lavish multicolored light and the room's darkness behind us. There the illumination is more constant, and Charlie loses his magnificent uniform, his Easter-egg head. Now he is a soft-white boy with an oblong, vulnerable face that is nebulously feminine and Norman Rockwell innocent. For a moment, in my eyes, he is simply my little brother.

Then he moves suddenly and looks up. "Sixty-two," he says, tapping at the total with the eraser of his pencil.

I am pleased with the total. "You must've had a rush at the end," I say.

"Probably coming from the movies," Charlie answers knowingly, and, from the sound of his voice, I think he is pleased also. Then, suddenly, he is adding and reading the figures, counting on his child-fingers, mumbling agedly. I am struck by the similarity of young and old, how Charlie is in one way twelve but, at the same time, the vision of the old man he may someday be, or, perhaps, already much of the old man he may someday be. There seems to be a homogeneity in child-fingers held like the partially flexible members of a rusted yard rake and the actual rusted joints of an imperfect old hand, and, though his utterances seem now to be simple mumbling, counting so his ears will help him add, they may someday be characterized as "talking to himself."

The figures total sixty-two again. Charlie scratches through the number. "What if I put ninety-seven?" he asks. "It's a good uneven number. Sounds authentic." Already he is erasing and changing items in the column. He needs no uniform for courage.

"Why not a hundred and seven?" I speculate.

Charlie laughs. "A hundred and seven is the number that got me caught today!"

"Cheating?"

"Yeah. I was copying Jan Funderburk's paper in Math. I sit behind her, and I put down a hundred and seven percent of the American population owns automobiles." He giggles at his imprudence. "God, how dumb can you get," he says and slaps his forehead. "Sometimes you can't trust girls to do anything right. Anyway, the principal believed her story over mine, and I got the licks."

I'm a little incredulous. "Her story?" I ask.

"Yeah."

"What then was your story? No, wait. You told him she was copying you."

"Yeah. And I could've won. I could've threatened Jan with our sex life, but then I'd have lost that." He is speaking like we are business associates. "I figured the licks were no big deal."

"But didn't she know you tried to lay it off on her?"

"Naw, the principal took us in his office separately. You know how they pull that crap on you. 'You tell me the truth and I'll go light on you.' They want to compare your stories. So I looked the bastard right in the eyes—you know how they tell you a liar always looks away. Well, I looked him right in the eyes and lied my ass off."

"Why'd he believe Jan then?"

"I heard him tell my teacher Jan was from a good family he'd been knowing for years, and he'd known her since the first grade and she'd never been in anything like that before."

I sense a slight annoyance when he says this.

"But," he continues, languidly gesturing with his small hands, then his shoulders, as if sloughing off this complication, "I'll just have to keep my mind on what I'm doing from now on."

I watch him a second; he is bright against the darkness of the room behind us. "So what are you going to put down for the total?" I ask.

Charlie smiles. "A hundred and seven," he triumphantly declares. There is little timidity in him, little capitulation.

I know then that Charlie understood from the beginning the ritual of his counting; he would count the cars as diligently, as systematically, as the rules required, but, if in the end the numbers were insufficient, he would manipulate the figures to his advantage, to our advantage. And I know, through Charlie, there is a distinct and unquestionable truth in the difference between cheating and survival. Counting cars is another campaign for Charlie; he has skirmished across the South, seven schools in six years. I have watched him battle on the schoolyards of four states, the new boy against the class bully, arms flailing in attack, and I have rescued him when he would not yield to injurious onslaughts, when his blood soaked beneath us into an earth not ours. I have listened in the night when his sleep was a torment of mutterings, a gibberish of combat, whimpers of woundings mixed with the staccato of his stertorous breath.

I think too that Charlie has come to understand that his real adversary is the restlessness of our father, this nomadic dreamer whose ghostly heart has trundled us through so many rental houses we have trouble remembering which house was where. I think this because it seems Charlie conceives he might, through his counting, give some direction to our destiny.

"A hundred and seven's a lot," I point out. "What if the old man has been downstairs counting?"

"You gotta take a chance sometimes," he answers. "If he still wants the grocery to do well, he'll take my numbers." Charlie says this resignedly which stirs my interest.

"If he still *wants* the grocery to do well," I repeat. "Why not?"

"Because the guy in the red Cadillac was here today."

There is suddenly a void within me, and I know Charlie has been feeling it also. The man in the red Cadillac gives new meaning to what we envisage as fate, something to which I have learned to succumb and even expect though I often force it from my mind, or, especially in the presence of Charlie, deny its existence. Usually there is an inevitability in my outlook; the years of impermanence have numbed the fear I used to feel for the man in the red Cadillac. I no longer fear him. It seems in the succession of events that I understand as life he is, or has become, an inescapable occurrence. The emptiness I feel is not from fear but resignation, the thing I heard in Charlie's voice, and I am afraid of that.

"Did you see him?" I ask.

Charlie nods, the light we sit in striking his feminine face as a faint siren sounds far off. There are soft hues of green, purple, and red between us and the window.

"I crawled in behind the fish box when they went into the office. I tried listening on the wall with a Mason jar, but my ear was better."

"What'd he say?"

"A lot of bullshit to begin with," he replies. "You know how the old man gets. The guy had a bottle and they had a few. Then they had to go over old times with all that 'Do you remember this; do you remember that?'"

There is the muted sound of a cash register being cleared. It comes from beneath us, and both of us start to rise instinctively.

"Then," Charlie continues, "they got to talking about all the money to be made in Florida selling some kind of machine that makes hamburger patties. Last time it was soft-serve ice cream machines."

"I know. We've got eighteen cases of that mix stuff in the basement right now and the rats love it."

"Yeah," he agrees. "Anyway, you-know-who must have had some kind of books on the machines, and they looked at those a little while. The money's what kept getting the old man. They figured out some deal to finance the machines—the guy has got some 'millionaire' putting up the money."

I really don't need to hear anymore.

But Charlie goes on. "After the guy left, the old man spent the afternoon slapping Mother on the tail. You know how he gets. He's playing around, falling all over himself, and she knows why. He's just getting her ready. She never says a word. Oh she'll cry like hell when it comes time to leave, but she really can't stand up to him. He even started it with me. Wanted to know if I'd like for us to go fishing in the ocean and what I thought about us having a swimming pool. You know how he primes you."

From his sock Charlie retrieves a Tootsie Roll, one of the small ones, and he holds it as if it is a cigar while biting bits from the end. He pinches it a time or two, it is mashed from being in his sock. "I was supposed to get a motorcycle," he says, "when we moved here. This store owes me a motorcycle."

15

I reach for the Tootsie Roll, take it out of his hand, and bite off half of it before he takes it back.

"We should go down," I suggest," and help them close-up," but neither of us moves to do it.

"A Harley's just got the sound. Know what I mean?" He studies what's left of the Tootsie Roll. "Does something to you kinda spiritual."

The Tootsie Roll tastes a little like fish.

"Maybe the old man knows," he continues, "a Harley could take me away from here." He says it like he's talking to himself, moves over to the window, looks out, and comes back to the chairs. He begins to circle with his pencil over the figures on his yellow pad. It's an aimless pencil-wondering.

"Where would you go, Charlie?"

He shrugs. "Maybe France. I've always wanted to ride a Harley around the Eiffel Tower." His pencil makes half-a-dozen lines in the shape of the Eiffel Tower.

"You sound like the old man."

"Crap you say! I decide where I go. No guy in a red Cadillac has to come by and make up *my* mind."

"But you're still going."

"Maybe we can't help it," he says angrily.

"What about the store?"

"You've seen the chart in the office," he says, pointing to the store beneath us. "I've got it going. I mean we're doing enough business to stay here. He sits there next to it and lets the guy in the red Cadillac ruin it all."

There are footsteps on the stairs down the hall. We can tell it's the old man by the slow tread on each step and the way he pushes each foot into a step, a sliding, grinding of grit. Some of the planks suffer under his large body, and we hear their complaints. At the top of the stairs he stops for a second, then comes across the hall to our door. We hear his great hand searching the wall for the lightswitch, and suddenly we are blinking in the brightness of a four tube fluorescent light that hangs above us.

"Sitting in the dark?" he asks. He puts his hands in his pockets and pulls them out several times as he walks to us. Then he rubs both sides of his stomach; he has ulcers. At almost six and a half feet tall and well over two hundred, he seems to fill the room. He smells of gin.

Charlie stands up. "I'll go chart the figures," he says, but the old man's hand takes hold of his shoulder and pushes him back to the chair.

"How would you guys like a swimming pool?" he asks while rubbing a balled-up fist over Charlie's head. "I mean in the backyard where you could jump in whenever you got hot." He begins shaking a long finger, hesitating, thinking, as if he's an actor portraying a sudden illumination and sorting it into words. His eyes are wide and a little red. "And fishing. A place where we could be fishing in the ocean in fifteen minutes." He paces. "I've been thinking about a place," he continues as Charlie rolls his eyes at me and looks away, "where we could do that. . . ."

"What about the cars?" Charlie interrupts, holding forth the yellow pad, and I see the rapid pulsation of his heart in the vessels of his neck. "I got a pretty good total!"

But the old man isn't concerned. "We'll get it tomorrow," he says, and I know, from the sound of his voice, from his look, that the charting, the pains of counting have come to nothing. Something sinks within me like a rock in a cold pond.

Charlie jumps to his feet, ever Jack, ever Napoleon, "I'll put it on the chart now," he almost shouts which seems to surprise the old man, but again the large hand holds his thin shoulder.

"I could teach you guys to shoot fish. You really got to be good to hit flounder. Good eye. Hell, I could have you guys popping fish in no time."

Charlie is beginning to cry. I notice his chin trembling. He pushes the yellow pad at the old man. "A hundred and ninety-two!" he shouts. "We never counted so many!"

The old man takes the pad and walks with it to the window where the blinking sign splays onto him. Then he tosses the pad on Charlie's bed in the corner of the room.

"Popping fish!" he exclaims, clapping his large hands.

"A hundred and ninety-two!" Charlie protests.

They stood there, both caught now in the various colors coming through the window, green, purple, red, dressed magically in the circus colors of our nomadic lives.

That night:
I dream the school will not hold us, that we
are too many, I fight a bulbous boy
in a red shirt, whacking his crew-cut head,
a boy with the face of a boy who laughed
at the tumult sucking us away.
I lose Charlie in the flooding melee
of fish children. I had his small white hand
in my palm, strange that I could feel it,
but we are at fingertips over bodies
schooling towards an exit where a grassless
playground is a beach to be washed upon
and where Charlie is carried from me.
There are thousands and thousands of children
all clamoring at the feet of an iron
sculpture, a giant's spindly monkey bars,
where one might climb higher from earthly floods
had one the daring, and it is there I
spot Charlie, highest of the thousands beached
in choiceless births—Charlie, the better of
our womb, waving silently, absurdly free.
The glove of sleep loosens its mythical
embrace. I open my eyes to darkness.
Charlie's dim ghost moves, fully dressed, across
the black room to the door beyond which is the
hall above the stairs that lead into the night.
He slips from me, a burglar stealing himself.

High into his mental beanstalk, Charlie stops,
hanging pendulously by one holding
while taunting from his dangerous aerie
those timid followers who have discovered
fear. He is the highest of the high.
I hold to an iron leg growing from the
ground, authenticating my fear of all
the deaths I must die, and Charlie sees me
amid the fish children. His voice is but

a hole in his face until I climb the first
and second rungs. "France!" he exclaims, and again,
"France!" He climbs higher and takes with him
his invitation to challenge the bars,
to leave the sea. I watch his small body
go into the blinking clouds, of green, purple,
and red, clouds that gather round him and rain
broken yellow numbers onto my heart.

A Solitary Journey

Jim lay in the ditch, hurting. He watched the new light on the pine tops and knew the sun would be up soon. There was a sharp pain in his lower back and it laced itself down the back of both legs. He could move his feet and he picked up his knees, but there was too much pain then to try and walk.

He remembered seeing the single red dot of light from the caboose as it sped away. There had been no sound and he wondered if it were because there really was no sound or because he had injured his head. He felt around his hair and found a wet spot behind his right ear. He snapped his fingers beside each ear and he could hear. He had been carrying a canvas Army bag with two handles when he fell, and he looked but could not see it. Then he felt it beneath him. How he had fallen upon it he did not know. He could only remember it leaving his hand when his feet went.

It had been a foolish thing to do. In fact, he'd never done it before, but lately he'd become too sure of himself and had taken the risk. At Hamlet he'd picked up the Seaboard Coast Line freight heading east to the coast. He'd heard there would be ships at the coast. Luckily he'd hopped a chemical car, and he'd crawled into the small space where the tank curved away from the frame. The space was big enough to sit and there were bracings to hold to and if you were brave you could buckle your belt around a bracing and sleep. This night he'd gotten cold, and, remembering an empty chip car up ahead into which he could lower himself out of the wind, he'd climbed the ladder on the chemical car, and, holding the canvas bag away from himself, began crawling across the metal walkway on the car's top. When he'd stretched his neck, he had seen the chip car ahead, but the wind had been very strong and he had to keep his head down. Then he'd slipped. His hands had not been able to hold the metal walkway and the bag unbalanced him enough to shift his weight onto the curved, smooth top of the car. The only move he'd made to save himself was a last second push from the car. If he was going off, he'd wanted to go off as far from the wheels as possible.

So he could not have been out long, if at all, to remember the red light. Too, there seemed to be some recollection of the freight conductor hunched over in the caboose. Yes, he'd seen him, but there had been no sound. Since the beginning of the fall there had been silence. He'd come to earth unheard; the train had escaped in absolute quiet. He remembered two towns. They must have been Laurinburg and Lumberton, so he must be somewhere in the flat pine country of the coastal plain. There was nothing here but miles of pines and scrub oaks and rattlesnakes. He shivered. Damn, he didn't want to die, not here, not now. The pain wasn't so much that he couldn't bear it, but he was afraid if would take too long. He tried to rest his head against the bank. He didn't want to lie here for days. If he was going to die, let it happen now. He tried to remember what he was carrying that he could use to kill himself. There was the penknife in the pants pocket of his fatigues, but when he felt for it he discovered the pocket torn away. The knife and part of his money were gone. He didn't need the money if he was going to die, but he missed the knife. The knife could have helped him.

Then he was very ill. He retched and vomited into the ditch. His lips felt very cold, but his cheeks were too warm and there was nausea that began in his stomach and radiated into his legs and arms. So, he thought, death would have its due, and he even laughed a little that it had come to this.

He vomited again and rolled away from it and tried to feel himself. But then he was sinking and there was no coming back. Pushing his head forward into the sand, he felt strange, narcotic-like sinking and knew death was easier than he'd imagined. It was like the tonsillectomy and the three operations on his arm. They had used ether then—back in the old days, and he laughed again that he'd reached a time when he could think it. There'd been a cool, damp swelling high up in his nose as the ether was breathed in and then there had been counting and always a nurse saying count and he could see her and her hand over his nose and mouth and he counted only a few numbers before they wouldn't come anymore and he was sinking. It was like that now only he was alone and he didn't want to be alone. He wished someone was there telling him to count. Count back from a hundred, he thought, and by the eighties you'll know—know if you've lived for something or nothing. You'll know before the eighties if it's all a lie, and for the third time he laughed, or thought he did, that he did not fear his own death now that he was with it.

Too many people came, too many for one room, but he was pushed toward the front and there was his grandfather, the great head sunk in the satin pillow. He didn't want to remember that. Everything about his grandfather was his alone and belonged to no one and he would think of his grandfather when the people had gone. He came back to the counting and the feeling just before he couldn't get the numbers anymore, but it wouldn't stay and he let it go. No need, no need now. Maybe the train didn't go too fast through here and someone would see him. No need to hold on to the numbers now.

When the sea came he was ready for it. First it was the whales at Isle of Palms. There were seven of them, huge black beauties that had beached themselves, their blow holes puffing slow death and he could do nothing. He had spoken to them when he was there alone and finally he had just made sounds and touched them. They had died and a bulldozer had come and pulled them off to a newly-dug ditch. For days he had watched for more but no more had come, and he had gone in the inlets and estuaries along the Intercoastal Waterway to watch the porpoises slither up the mud flats at low tide. Why had the whales not flopped themselves back into the water as the porpoises? He wondered if the whales were watching now, and he hoped they were.

Then the ocean was much deeper and he was shrimping again. It felt good to be back on the deck of the Mary Lou. They had come out of Shem Creek into Charleston Harbor on the Cooper River side with Shutes Folly Island off to starboard and Fort Sumter ahead. It was not yet dawn and the warning lights of Sullivan's Island blinked as the shrimper rounded to the northeast. He could smell the coffee in the little pilot house and someone called him, perhaps Snake Eyes, the captain, but then he could not find the voice and the Mary Lou was gone.

But the ocean was there and he was going way out, out farther than he'd ever been, and after awhile there were islands he knew he should recognize but couldn't. As he drew closer he saw their names in the sand of their beaches. One was Guadalcanal, then there were New Georgia and Choiseaul and Bougainville—names he'd known all his life, but he had never been there. His father had been there and never returned, and as the islands came under them he realized he was flying with his father in the P-40 and they were counting off the

22

islands. His father spoke with the crackling static of far-off radio transmission, and he had a big smile on his face that seemed to push his earphones upwards on his head. Past Bougainville there was a huge expanse of ocean, beautiful blue-green water, and Jim could see the whales down below in the water. They spouted water like some kind of code. His father was pointing ahead and he heard his voice say, "New Britain," and after awhile his father turned and handed him the stick. "Rabaul," his father said. "It's not as hard as we make it out to be," and the plane was going down so he let go the stick and thought about his father and the whales. He was sinking but he had found his father and the whales were waiting.

The warmth turned to a sweaty hot and several flies were on his face and there was an old man talking to a dog. The old man sat on the rail, his thin knees forming a V over which his unshaven face kept looking back at him after shouting at the dog. ". . . your putrid soul!" Jim heard the old man yell. The dog, a large gray mongrel, hunched down his head on his paws and sprang in the air at the old man's voice.

The old man watched Jim. "He's a puppy yet," he said. "Thinks I'm playing."

Jim brushed the flies away.

"Almost noon. You been lying there a long time."

Jim could not remember where he was for a second, but the rails brought back the night before. Then the pain was with him again and he looked at his legs and they were straight enough, but the right one ached like an impacted tooth and when he moved his head he pulled the hair dried against his scalp and neck. There was a dull humming in his right ear. The tracks ran straight away in both directions. The rock bed was almost white in the sun, and it hurt his eyes to look at the old man. He pushed himself up a little and managed to work his bag free from beneath him.

"Couldn't tell anything's broken," said the old man. "Arms and legs felt all right. Bad place on your head. How you feel in the middle?"

"Sore," he answered. He rubbed his hands over his ribs and there was no pain.

"Thought you were dead at first. Couldn't see you breathing till I held a cigarette to your mouth."

"I don't feel much alive," Jim said.

23

"Jump off the train?"

"Fell."

The old man stood slowly. He carried a long walking stick, and he held tightly to it as he limbered his legs. He carefully came down the gravel embankment of the railroad and approached Jim. "The dog turned this up," he said handing Jim the plastic-wrapped money.

He thanked the old man and told him there had been a knife, but the old man shook his head.

"Thanks for this anyway. It's all till I can get something at the coast," he lied—there was more in his left sock, but he was unsure of the old man and he was hurt.

Fishing in his pocket, the old man came out with a roll of hard candy. "Eat a few of these. It'll have to be your breakfast."

The candy was sweet and good and made him feel alive. He tried to hand the roll back, but the old man would not take it. Then, while the old man held the walking stick firmly to the ground, Jim pulled himself up. He tried the right leg but the pain was too much to put weight on it.

"Put your arm around my shoulder," said the old man, "and take the stick with the other hand." He picked up Jim's bag and took a tight grip at his waist. "We'll make it a ways like this. Couple of miles to my place but we got all day."

The old man was strong and he hefted Jim most of the first half mile before they stopped to rest. They had crossed a small trestle over slow-moving water, black water that had reflected them and the thick creosote pilings and a singular cloud that had looked to Jim like a buffalo.

"Goes over to the Cape Fear River," the old man pointed out. "Good thing you didn't fall there, hit the pilings or drown."

Jim stretched out his right leg." If I'd stayed where I was, I wouldn't have fallen at all."

The old man laughed for the first time. "Probably ain't a man alive couldn't say that. Smoke?"

He took a cigarette and shared the old man's match. He hadn't smoked in a long time and he took three or four deep drags, sucking the smoke deep in his lungs, and made himself a little dizzy and the pain lessened. "I'm Jim Dillon," he said shifting his weight to one elbow.

"I seen your name on the Army bag."

"That's my father. We've got the same name."

"Good thing to do. My name's Monroe Shaw. My father's name was Fuquay Shaw, but my grandfather was a Monroe. At least his last name." Monroe put his hand out and they shook. "I knew a Dillon once a long time ago," he continued. "Killed three men down in Georgia—killed a woman too. Anyway, they strung him up in the bell steeple of a church."

Jim managed a smile but the pain was increasing. "No kin that I know of. You live in Georgia?"

"Used to travel around some. Had a hard time getting settled. Got a little place in the woods now. Fish when I want, hunt when I want, and get drunk when I want. Don't wander around no more. Too many people."

When Jim tried to get up, his head began spinning and the nausea rolled in his stomach. He sank to the ground.

"Put your head between your knees," said Monroe and when he did the fainting went away.

After another cigarette Monroe pulled him up and they struggled another quarter of a mile before turning down a path and into the pines where it was cooler. The dog ran ahead, sniffing the trail and disappearing only to come back from the right or left, zigzagging in his infantile hunt, getting a scent and losing it, attracted by every movement, every sound. Because of the pain Jim was sure they had been walking for at least two hours, but it had only been thirty minutes, and when they stopped to rest again, he sat on his bag to keep from getting chiggers in the pine straw and folded his arms over his left knee as a headrest. When the dog ran off the pines were very quiet, and he was feeling better out of the direct sun. Monroe helped him remove his right boot, and it eased the pain that now seemed lodged in his hip. The foot was slightly swollen and had turned blue along the ankle. Monroe gently rotated it. There was not much pain and it moved okay and Jim felt very good that it was not broken.

"Must've hit on your right leg," Monroe said.

"I wish I could remember. It's like it was all a dream you know you had but can't remember."

"Looks like you hit on the right foot then the back of your head. Too bad you weren't drunk. Can't hurt drunks. You'd have got up and walked off."

Jim studied Monroe's face and build. In the cool light of the pine

25

forest, Monroe didn't look like an old man. His face, neck and hands were wrinkled, but his shoulders were square, the neck thick, and his blue eyes were undimmed and filmless and they were not watery. When he lit cigarettes his hands were steady.

Monroe put the boot in the Army bag. "Where you from?" he asked.

"Greensboro. Left out thumbing. Caught the freight in Hamlet when night came. I heard I could get a ship on the coast."

Nodding, Monroe said, "You got a Seaman's Card? You'll have to have one."

"Why?"

"To get a ship. You'll have to go down to the union hall and put in for a Seaman's Card. Then you'll go on the sailing list according to trade."

He had no trade. He was two hands and two feet and fairly strong—until now. Now he needed a doctor and maybe a hospital and the coast seemed very far away.

After two more hours they came to Monroe's place in the woods. It was a clearing that was swept clean, no grass, no weeds. In the middle was a burned trailer and only the chassis remained. Between the blackened chassis and a dirt road was a twenty-year-old Cadillac without wheels, standing on cement blocks.

"Got drunk and burned my trailer down," Monroe explained good humoredly. "Been living in my car."

Monroe propped him against the Cadillac's front fender. From beneath the burned trailer chassis he pulled a metal frame cot with springs stretched across it. He took newspapers from the Cadillac's back seat and spread them over the cot and put a blanket over the papers. He placed the cot next to a fireplace around which were rocks. There was a screen over the rocks and a blackened coffee pot on the screen.

He eased Jim onto the cot and carefully stretched out his legs. "This will hold you straight enough in case your back's hurt. Mail man'll be by in the morning and we'll get you in to the hospital."

Jim thanked him.

Monroe built a fire and put on pork and beans, Vienna sausages, and coffee. From the trunk of the Cadillac he brought out a bottle of Canadian whiskey and filled two coffee cups half full. Then he poured in the coffee. After the first cup Jim felt the pain become dull, a warm aching that the whiskey diluted and spread over his body. He ate, and he drank another cup and napped, and for awhile the pain was very far away. When he woke it was dark and he was hungry again, so Monroe heated more pork and beans and fried two large slabs of country ham he cut from a ham in the trunk. They drank more of Monroe's coffee.

"Means you're gonna live," Monroe said.

"What?"

"Eating. Anybody eat two cans of pork and beans by himself got to be feeling pretty good." He smiled across the fire.

"Nothing wrong with my stomach. Wish my leg felt as good."

"Drink your coffee."

The fire lit Monroe's face. He was golden then and the skin below his eyes sagged a little from the whiskey, and after the first cup his voice had become hoarse. He sat in a wooden chair with the Cadillac behind him.

The cot kept Jim's body flat which, along with the whiskey, relaxed his muscles and allowed his blood to circulate evenly. When he looked to his left he could see Monroe across the fire, to his right was the burned trailer, and above him was the great lake of the night edged all around by the dark pine tops. The night was clear and the stars seemed very close to the pine tops. He had heard the train when they were eating the second time, and it had vibrated the cot even when it was far away. "Nine-thirty," Monroe had said when they heard it.

"It's a good place to be, Monroe."

"I like it."

"Ever been better?"

Monroe fixed another whiskey and coffee while he thought. "There were times in the war," he finally said. "We thought they weren't good times but they were."

"Where were you?"

"Pacific."

"My father was there."

"Well he had some good times, Jim. We all did. And we've got a lot of good things to think about. Your father tell you about the good times?"

27

"He didn't come back. I never saw him." Jim drank the whiskey and watched the sky.

"What was his outfit?"

"He was a pilot."

"I was infantry. . . . We had some good times." Monroe stared into the fire. "Flyboys had some good times too. He would've done a lot of living, Jim. He would've seen more than most men do in a long lifetime and I guarantee he would've had some good times."

Jim looked at Monroe and watched him sway as the whiskey soothed him.

"I think sometimes," he continued, "it's the ones didn't come back were the luckiest. I mean they climbed the mountain and they stayed there. Never had to come down."

Jim rolled back and watched the sky again. "You remember your father, Monroe?"

There was a silence of several seconds before Monroe answered. "Yeah. I get out here all alone and sometimes I think I hear him. I get to imagining things like when I was a kid, you know, like people around you. Hell, I even talk sometimes." He chuckled huskily.

Then he sat forward and spit in the fire. "Don't know about you, Jim, but I'm drunk as a skunk and if I don't get to bed I just might pass out in this fire." He stood unsteadily, pulled the chair away from the fire, and opened the rear door of the Cadillac. "Here," he said coming back. "Put this sleeping bag over your legs. It may get cool before morning. You're gonna be stiff as a board anyway, but it'll go away." He started toward the Cadillac, returned, and began stacking wood next to the cot. "Throw this on if you need it," and, finally, "Goodnight." Then he crawled slowly into the back seat.

Jim lay for a long while watching the sky and letting his mind go where it would, and, when the last of the whiskey was finished, he put his left arm over his forehead and prayed. He prayed for his family and for Monroe Shaw and for the pain. He prayed for someone he loved and he prayed for his father. He prayed that his father had had good times and had been up the mountain. Then he breathed deeply for a few minutes and tried to feel the whiskey more than the pain and just before he slept he thought he opened his eyes to the night sky and saw the whales. There were seven of them and they were beautiful and when they surfaced the water around them was white and they were blue and as they began to disappear beyond the dark pine tops he thought he heard the singular drone of an aircraft as it followed them. Then he slept and he did not think anymore.

Meat of the Dead

My name. My name. Warm syrup round me, flowing down from my straw hair, down my shoulders, my hips. My feet are heavy in the ooze of my name, standing me here on the two joists of the unpainted back porch, the flooring gone, and I look between my warm legs to the red earth for my name, and my name, my name comes again but not from beneath my legs, from away, away, away to the other side of the earth—over at the hog pen. My name again and it is a new-born kitten I have brought from the highway in my coat with a Coke and potato chips, and its name is my name though no one knows but Jesse Daddy.

Careful in the syrup. Careful kitten. Jump! Fly like the old turkey, the gobble-giggle. No one can fly like the gobble-giggle but me because I gobble-giggle my mouth full of air and go over the wooden steps. I hold my jaws steady and my cheeks bulge like mushrooms are growing in my teeth, and I glide out into my name. No one up here where I fly but my name, not dead James, not the goddamn big red hog, not the test-giver, not the school bus, not the niggers—not nobody can gobble-giggle air like I can and fly except my name, my warm name.

Jesse Daddy. "Here, Purdy." Coming, but I won't run like the gobble-giggle because I run like the white duck that got chewed-up by wild dogs. My feet are duck feet. Even at recess my feet are duck feet and I cannot gobble-giggle enough air or hold my arms straight enough for my feet not to be duck feet. One is crazy and I go crooked, but I'm coming to you Jesse Daddy, coming crooked with my head down so I won't know when I'm to you until you uncrook me with your plaid shirt that smells like breakfast. I'm coming to my name.

Three hogs in the roof-tin pen, rusted roof tin from the chicken coop and a gone turkey and a gone duck—nailed to chinaberry trees with roots snouted-out like duck ribs. Three hogs. Two of them are not there over the rust beneath my fingers; only the goddamn big red hog is there in my eyes and he shoots stink at me trying to stink-up my name. The goddamn big red hog chews on my feet in the night, swallowing me sometimes to my knees, and I know if I go to its belly I could not call Jesse Daddy—I could not remember my name in the hollow of its stink belly.

Jesse Daddy. "Git!" but the goddamn big red hog doesn't move. With no name it can't hear deep in its stinkmeat; so Jesse Daddy pokes it with a hoe handle and whack! then. And whack! again. Maybe Whack is the name of the goddamn big red hog.

Me. "Git, Whack!" I feel better. I am not afraid when I yell. "Whack! Whack! Whack!" and Jesse Daddy smiles as good as calling my name. "Goddamn big hog Whack! Goddamn sausage ass!" I say, and Jesse Daddy hands me the hoe handle, but I cannot reach so I spit over my fingers.

Jesse Daddy. "We gonna git that goddamn big red hog," he says in my eyes, "ain't we, Purdy? We gonna grind his sausage ass for breakfast!"

Me. "Grind his meat now." Grind it before it can come again in the quiet night behind my eyes, come and swallow me away where I can't never hear my name. "Goddamn sausage ass!" I say from Jesse Daddy's arms where the goddamn big red hog ain't never coming because Jesse Daddy calls my name, and nothing can get me when he calls my name.

I look in Jesse Daddy's ear, but I don't see dead James; I don't see my name, but it is there deep inside of him, so I sing "Jesse Loves Me" like I used to sing "Jesus Loves Me," sing it to Jesse Daddy and to my name. I changed the words because Jesus does not know about goddamn big red hogs, about how they can swallow in the night. Jesus ain't never let me whack a hog, and He ain't never told me, told me with His head under the covers, I could stay home from school when the test-giver was coming with pages of words I don't know because they ain't my name and pegs I can't fit nowhere because they ain't big enough to whack a hog. Goddamn pegs and goddamn hogs—but Jesse Daddy's ear is big enough for me to put my name in, big enough to sing in, and Jesse Daddy's shirt smells like breakfast. I ain't never smelled Jesus.

From the back porch. "Jesse." It ain't my name, but it feels as good as my name, feels like riding in the floorboard of the back seat of the car with the heater blowing under the seat. The name is from my mother who has a bucket for Jesse Daddy, and he goes for it, leaving me alone by the pen, alone with the goddamn big red hog.

Me. "I prayed to Jesus you'd die." It raises its head, able to hear
only me because I have found out its name. "Now I pray to Jesse
you'll die, you goddamn big red grind ass, you Whack." I back away
from the rusted tin. "Jesse Daddy will kill you and I will eat your
meat and I will never have to go to school again and dead James will
be happy to see you hang by your hind legs from the chinaberry and
Mother will fry your meat for breakfast. I won't be the only white
girl on the bus no more because I ain't going. All you got to do is die.
And you leave my name alone."

My mother follows Jesse Daddy to me. She is an old woman,
thirty her last birthday—too many candles for a cake so dead James
wrote out 30 in the numbers with red icing and put one candle
between them and I ate the 0, or the top of it, and I got up in the
night to escape the goddamn big red hog in my bed and went to the
kitchen and sat at the yellow table and ate icing. That was the night
James followed me and told me he had decided to grow up and be a
rich farmer and eat steak. He said when he died it'd be like the
president was dead and people would come from all over and the
newspapers would have his name on the first page. It turned out to
be a lie.

My mother is wearing Jesse Daddy's jacket with the sleeves rolled
up so her hands will stick out. She squints up at the morning sun,
over the chinaberries, and I see the gone tooth, not the front one but
the one next to the one next to the front one; a dentist pulled it for
twelve dollars, a gone tooth, gone like dead James, a hollow place.
My mother is smoking and when she speaks smoke gossamers her
words as if she is on fire inside, burning up her meat, like when I get
up early for school and forget and call dead James and my words
frost out of my mouth so that I can see them, and I know I am there,
freezing away my meat, and that James' side of the bed is only
covers. My mother says we are going to the store for boxes; we are
moving again.

My mother. "What did they bring?"

Jesse Daddy. "Thirty apiece. I'll kill the red un and take it with
us."

It is said, made into words, and the words go through me.

Me. "Can we kill the goddamn big red hog today?" and my
mother spits when I say Jesse Daddy's word.

32

Jesse Daddy. "Kill the goddamn big red hog right now, Purdy."
Laughing. My name. His meat must never burn up or freeze inside
because my name always comes from him as though it has been
there, in a very good place, waiting, since before I was born, and
what are evil words to my mother come from Jesse Daddy like he
made them up and they are his, and I wonder if maybe they are really
his, really, and if he made the world up too.

So it is here. So dead James will be happy. So I won't go to school.
So I won't ride the bus with the niggers; so I will never again be the
only white girl on the bus. So we will eat the meat, the goddamn big
red hog meat, and never be swallowed again, not me, not dead
James, not my mother, not Jesse Daddy.

There is a white duck in me and I run. I feel my body going
crooked, but I know the world is round, round from the woods
beyond the soybean field to the hog pen to the front yard and the
highway; so I will come back to this place again. My run is around
the unpainted house, the house perched on cement blocks, the house
that never smells right except when my mother is frying meat—
around the corner to the front yard and the screen door that is against
the weeping willow and then the bed of cannas I have never bothered
because they are my mother's. Now I run through them; we are
moving. I stop once to gobble-giggle more air in case I need to fly. I
spin with my mouth open and the wind pushes my cheeks and I
remember to cover my bad tooth with my tongue as the white duck
pounds its wings in my ears; its wings are saying my name, my
name.

Leaving that side of the world, I run along the house where the
kitchen pipe, a black plastic pipe, comes from the side of the house as
though it were a black arm to catch me, but I fly over it and hold my
breath so I cannot smell the rotting food from the kitchen sink that
has washed out of the black pipe. Dead James shot a rat there once,
sneaked the rifle out the window—we did not even breathe, and as I
plugged my ears and heard the white duck beating its wings my
brother pulled the trigger and I felt his finger go all the way through
me. The rat flew into the air, flew like a string had jerked it, flew like
nothing I have ever seen fly before, and, before feeding it to the
goddamn big red hog, James and I searched inside it for the bullet;
we separated its meat but there was no bullet. We searched in the

33

rotting beans and rice, but there was no bullet. James said the bullet had gone to China, to China covered with red rat's blood, and I remember that blood because it was the same as James' blood when they called us to the bridge and James' hand, the same hand had pulled the trigger, lying cut off on the pavement while the rest of him was under the truck, still on Willie Goss' motorcycle. The meat of the hand, James' gun hand, was pale, the color of wet-wood smoke, and, I hated to think it—hate to think it—the meat was the same as hog meat. I stood over the hog-meat hand and softly put my toe into the palm; it was then I knew the hand had killed a China-man.

But the black plastic pipe is behind me, behind my flight, gone forever for I promise myself never to go by it again; we are moving. When the Chinamen get here we'll be gone.

I come to the unpainted back porch and wrap my arm around a cat-scratched post and peek my head under the boards looking for the kitten with my name. My ears hear Jesse Daddy's steps coming through the house. He is coming with death. I know; he has promised. When I pull my head out, he is there, coming through the door with the rifle held low in one hand, tilting him as though death was heavy.

The first shot is in the head, a hole below the goddamn big red hog's eye, and it wobbles, the head wobbles, then quivers as if its meat is freezing inside. Its front legs begin to come toward us, stepping unsurely, stepping like Jesse Daddy coming in late in the night, and in my ears are the beating duck wings; the rifle has not killed the goddamn big red hog and it is coming to swallow me away from Jesse Daddy and my name. It is filling my eyes. It is shooting its stink in my nose, and my ears have gone away already, gone with dead James where there is no sound, no names, no warm syrup of names. Though I can no longer hear I know I am screaming Jesse Daddy's name, hoping my name will come from deep within him and save me; only Jesse Daddy can save me.

The second shot is without sound; it is only a whiff of dust on the goddamn big red hog's head, a whiff of answered prayer, and the fat, quivering thing falls slowly to its left, crippled—like one crippled step could not hold it in this world, salvation gone forever like the rat's flight and, maybe, like James' last grasp or the deafness within me where the duck wings have vanished and left the silence I know is the real me—no one knows but me, real because I have felt my own meat quiver; I have felt the silent plodding of my heart toward death, walking after James, and I have felt my feeble heart swell and race to Jesse Daddy for salvation. I wonder if a pig has a heart.

Jesse Daddy is picking me up, although I am too big, as long as the goddamn big red hog lying dead before us, as he is wiping my face and calling softly to me, my name, my name from Jesse Daddy, and I understand then that I have not stopped screaming his name since the firing of the rifle, since the beginning of death. The deafness slowly leaves me, pushed out by my name, and I am suddenly happy; the goddamn big red hog is dead and I am safe.

The jelly-meat hog is lifted with a pully strung from the china-berry. He inches up by his hind legs until his dripping head is a foot off the ground and his forefeet sway above the chinaberry roots. Jesse Daddy cuts the goddamn big red hog from between its hind-legs, down its belly, and into its chest, and stink snakes ooze out onto the newspapers my mother has spread beneath. In the cool air the stink snakes are steaming. Each jab of the bloody knife gurgles in the quaking flesh and more snakes come out along with other parts I do not know but which seem to be the heads of children the god-damn big red hog has swallowed. Did it feed on James? I am afraid to look, but I cannot help myself. Jesse Daddy pulls the sides of the belly back, and I see where the goddamn big red hog was trying to swallow me, where it was trying to get my feet to go, and I chill-shake so that my lips press to one another like I got no teeth. More steam comes from its innards and I remember the church and I remember the Holy Hell and I remember the fires of the Holy Hell, and I know now that Holy Hell is inside the goddamn big red hog; I see the steam from Holy Hell; I know it is dark in there; I know it is where the unknown people go, like dead James who never got bap-tized and never got saved and killed a Chinaman. I know it is where Jesse Daddy will go because he says "goddamn" and uses tobacco and went to the drunkman's jail once, and I know I am going because Jesse Daddy is going and because "goddamn" feels good to me, almost as good as my name . . . unless Jesse Daddy is God. I remember he answers prayer, but it worries me that he did not save James. Yet, Jesse Loves Me begins in my head and it fits as good—no better—than anything has ever fit.

Jesse Daddy looks at me and says, "Chitlins," and his face is a rising moon and I know he is happy because James was not in the goddamn big red hog; I know the nights he has spent looking for my brother. But that is over now. There is something between us, something important; we will eat the goddamn big red hog. I have never believed it, not until now, not until I see the sidemeat Jesse Daddy is cutting away, but it is here, here between us. My mother will fry porkchops for breakfast and we will eat away the goddamn big red hog; things will be good again. Bacon will smell up the house—Jesse Daddy can eat a dozen slices easy—and my teeth will be a Holy Hell for the goddamn big red hog; things will be good again. Jesse Daddy will smile when I eat. Meat will be hung in the closet, hung there for the winter and for Christmas and New Year's when we eat ham and greens and blackeyes so we will have good luck and money the rest of the year. Things will be good again.

Jesse Daddy. "Push me the pan."

And I hold an aluminum dish pan beneath his steaming, bloody hands, his hands of snakes, drooping, hanging loose, too many snakes for two hands, and he laughs at my puckered lips. His chitlins, his stinking chitlins. This is meat I cannot eat, cannot bear to smell cooking. They come from the Holy Hell steaming, smelling like they smell cooking. My mother cuts into them and scrapes out the shit; "mess" she says, but I know it's shit, pig shit—the niggers call me white pig shit, and I believed them until today. I believed I was going to the Holy Hell and be pig shit until today. Now they are wrong. Now things will be good again.

The Holy Hell is open now, open to the world and school and the test-giver. Anyone can see dead James is not there, not even his cut-off hand is there, not even Mama's tooth is there, and I know my name has kept me from going there and my prayers to Jesse Daddy have kept me from being pig shit.

Knawing. Rat knawing in the night, but as my eyes come back to me I see it is Jesse Daddy's meat saw scraping across the goddamn-big-red-hog's ribs. Knaw. Knaw. Spareribs. Back and forth it is a song, and I am swinging on the saw. Back and forth I sing a song

36

they said I couldn't learn. They—the test-giver and the music teacher—don't know my words:

> Me. "Knaw, knaw on a old dead dog,
>   I done killed a big red hog.
>   Knaw, knaw tell my cat to git,
>   What you know 'bout bein pig shit?"

My words make me very happy. I stand and sway with my words and the white duck is happy within me. I sing better than I fly.

Jesse Daddy. "Who gonna fry up this goddamn-big-red hog, Purdy?" He says Purdy like God would say Purdy. He is God.

Jesse Daddy. "Who, Purdy?" when I don't answer.

Me. "You, Jesse Daddy. You gonna fry up the goddamn-big-red hog!" and none of us will go to Holy Hell my words say on inside of me. None of us.

My mother. "Purdy, don't let me hear that word from you no more," but she don't know Jesse Daddy is God and that the Holy Hell will leave us forever, soon as we fry up the goddamn-big-red hog. She has no meat on her bones and she ain't never been able to fly. She has a church God that she prays to and she prays for James to come back and she don't like me saying "goddamn" because it might make the church God mad and something worse than James' dying might come on us. She's been worried that James wasn't saved and I guess that's where the Holy Hell fits in, but looks like she could see he ain't there and it's a lie.

Jesse Daddy. "She don't mean nothing."

My mother. "'Thou shalt not take the name of the Lord thy God in vain.'"

Jesse Daddy. "We ain't really doin that."

My mother. "You think He don't hear?" pointing to the sky with a bloody knife.

But Jesse Daddy smiles at me and holds out his clutched hand and I know he's being God again and I look into his red fingers opening and there is an eyeball from Holy Hell, an eyeball looking at me, taking my eyes, staring away my breath.

Jesse Daddy. "Lookin at you, Purdy," laughing out my name from deep within his warm self so that my breath returns to my eyes. I am saved.

Digging into the hard, red dirt, the handle of my mother's spoon bends, but the hole is deep enough and I place the eyeball there, sunken-eyeball-into-the-earth, still watching me until I turn it toward China.

Me, whispering. "Watch Chinamen. Take their breath away." I am glad the eyeball has no mouth and cannot tell the Chinamen my name or where I'm going or where James is. "Scare the pig shit out of them," as I stick the eyeball with the spoon, stick it hard so it will hurt. Then I stick it again for James.

And Jesse Daddy has come from nowhere to stand beside me. In his hand is the other bloody eyeball and he drops it in my hole and touches me.

Jesse Daddy. "This too shall pass away," and perhaps, I think, he is talking about James, talking something I know his own mother has taught him—"This too shall pass away."—some kind of family thing, something, between us, the living and the dead. Yes, James and all the rest.

Jesse Daddy's hand is not so bloody that I'm afraid to hold it, and I do, from the ground up, and the blood stuck dirt on my hand sticks to him.

Someone is coming. A truck. A star on the side of the cab—where the sun shines off the metal—is winking at me, then hurting my eyes looking through me. I feel frightened that it knows my name, as my ears hear the black paws on the ground smashing pecans. Slowly pawing forward. I cover my hole with the same toe that touched James pig-meat hand; there are things we've put in the ground to hide.

A beatle-eyed man, Screppes, the unpainted house owner, the landowner is alone in the shining truck. He does not fit there, but he is there, and he does not get out—he never gets out here; he blows and we go to the truck. Through the windshield, where the china- berry trees reflect, he looks like a Chinaman, a round yellow face, but the eyes are too big and when I squint I see the pig fat on his jaws and neck. His eyes could be the eyes I've just buried. I hold my foot hard over the grave and say to myself he will have to kill me to get the eyes.

Screppes. "Talk to you a minute, Jesse," as Jesse Daddy wipes his hands on a newspaper and walks over to the opened window.

There is a white duck within me again. I don't know why. I don't know why when I see this man I know I am going to die. I don't know why but I know James saw this man just before he died. I don't know why but I know this man has something to do with the school bus and the test-giver. I don't know why—except that the white duck warns me—but I know this man has something to do with the goddamn-big-red hog and Holy Hell.

Jesse Daddy. "I was comin to see you this afternoon, Mr. Screppes," but his voice is not God's voice.

Screppes. "Thought we could do something about this," handing a paper to Jesse Daddy, "you leavin and all."

Jesse Daddy. "I mean to take care of it, Mr. Screppes, but I can't do nothin this morning" My name has never come from that voice.

My lips tighten over my teeth. My breath is almost gone in the white duck's beating. I smell pig shit.

Screppes. "Got to have something done about it now, Jesse. Seems like it's been long enough."

I wonder if my eyes are my own because I see James sneaking the rifle out the window. I have no breath. James, warm James, my brother is there in the white duck beating, there beyond me where my eyes have gone. The rifle is hovering, hovering, and the long, cold night haunting is in my chest, driven there by the white duck. I think I am flying, but it is unlike any flying I've ever done; it is as if I am two things, one staying, one going, and the going is like the gone white duck; it is gone forever—and, yet, it is here forever. I am going with James and I am staying with me. James has taken the rifle from the window, but his face is there and he is saying something to me. Perhaps it is "This too shall pass away." I don't know, but I feel some of my name is going with him. Then he is gone.

Jesse Daddy. "This afternoon I could do somethin," running out low across the ground, lying there.

Screppes. Head, huge head, shaking slowly. "Seems I've waited long enough. Got to be something done about it now. I just don't see no way but something be done about it now." In his forehead there are blood vessels jumping.

I pray Jesse Daddy will kill this man. I pray he will shoot him once below the left eye and once in his jumping blood vessels. In my eyes he is taking the rifle and, though there is no sound, I see a whiff of dust rise from Screppes' forehead, a death whiff. Screppes looks at me as if I have surprised him, as if in death he knows all of it and cannot believe Jesse Daddy is God. I am saying, "See what you have done to God."

Jesse Daddy. "I ain't got nothin but some furniture."

Screppes looks around our yard that is his yard. He takes in my mother.

My mind is saying, "Shoot! Please, God, shoot!"

Screppes. "How bout the hog yonder?"

Jesse Daddy. "I was plannin on hanging it for the winter, Mr. Screppes."

From the truck window there is spit, a splattering of brown that does not seem to want to soak into the ground. Pig shit. I am the only one who knows?

Screppes. "Cash or the hog, Jesse. This has gone far enough."

I think Jesse Daddy will go for the rifle. He moves. But my mother comes to the truck and sets her pan of stinking snakes in the back. Jesse Daddy watches her like he watched dead James carried away. I remember—like it ain't real, like he is drunk, like he's forgotten he is God, then he walks to the chinaberries, leans his shoulder against the hanging goddamn-big-red hog, and reaches up and unties the pully. The goddamn-big-red hog eases on him until I think he will fall from the tremedous weight, but he does not, only walks lower, his face the face of James in the window, his legs—his thin, drunken legs—only bending like legs that know they will never fly, never run straight. I look for his eyes but they have gone into himself. He comes from one end of the world with what's left of my name within him, and he slowly—as though he were carrying dead James—goes to the truck and lays the goddamn-big-red hog there.

My mother chunks in the sidemeat that was sawed away, and it is done. She stands to the other side of the truck behind Jesse Daddy, and her thin hand, coming from his rolled-up jacket like it is his own shrunken self, holds to his shirt. They stand at the other end of the world, far off from me.

The truck leaves and I move to the bloody killing spot that is now only blood.

My name. My name comes. Again it comes. From the other end of the world, as far as I've ever been or will ever go, comes my name, looking for me. It comes into me as always, comes fluttering with wings—comes from Jesse Daddy, but there is not enough of my name left within him for times to be good again. I would die for him. Right now I would die to save him from the anguish of my name.

TURNER CASSITY

Advice to King Lear

Arneson River Theatre, on the San Antonio River,
is the most unique of the city's theatres. On
one side of the river are tiers of grass seats;
on the other a patio-type stage. Occasional passing boats enhance audience enjoyment.

San Antonio; a Pictorial Guide

Unlikely in the semi-desert, azure
Night, the storm out on the heath is seizure
In the King's own madness. It is pressure
On the backers for a quick foreclosure.
Verse or wind machine, the awful matter
Finds its vehicle and has its stutter.

As if the footlights floated off in glitter,
Pleasure craft now part the placid water.
The onstage weather every act is glummer;
Outdoors or in, a mummer's still a mummer;
Your fool can only grow forever dumber.
Heirs? They march one to their different drummer.
Get on the boat, Old Man, and go to summer.

Gun of the Moon

Inertly rusting in its well of fire-brick,
Covered, but itself a cistern dense
With the mosquitoes of the many years
Since it was fired, the moon gun breeds its wings
And draws its tourists—memory and quinine
Strong, ex-future passed to pestilence.

"*Columbiad*, the gun from which, on July
4th of 1866, was shot
Man's first projectile from the Earth to Moon.
'A fuse length for a man, and for his kind
The ages' dream. How long the leagues of light?'"
But for the plaque, and for the rays of scorch

Upon the level ground of oyster shell,
It might seem what it is: a wishing well,
A fountain rim mute in a quiet garden.
Goddess, in the canvas-covered deep,
Your image, unreflected, measures Earth.
Red, far below the rotting tarpaulin,

Two fevers mock at Eratosthenes.
And one is you, whose tense and crescent arc
Is for the primal arrow primal bow.
The missile will connect or will fall short;
The well of our ambition will not change.
Eternal each, gun cotton and the Moon,
Event and consequence, the blast, the pest.

TURNER CASSITY

The Incorruptible
(Kansas City)

A lot of Sodom in a little rain,
Sin's most accomplished City of the Plain
Sits on its ridge. A high school band in tow,
I doze on board a school bus. How atone,
Who am the world's last living chaperon.
Hotel rooms—eight—the boys on one and two,

The girls on high floors undisclosed, and pray
Their elevators fail. Though I must pay
For steak, thereafter they are on their own,
The shy to search the nearest pusher out,
The bold to stammer, at the hooker. Rout
Or triumph, harder rain must send them home,

Free, wet; and poker on the second floor
Be all their sin. It keeps us up till four.
Tomorrow, on a pristine Astro Turf,
In uniforms that are a bright echo
Of Österreich-Ungarn, a heartland show,
They will compete for two weeks in the surf,

And, being sleepy, lose.
                                    Outside of town
The Zoar local overheats, breaks down.
It is a judgment. In the endless halt
To change the hoses they do not look back.
There is no fire, no brimstone; only wreck,
And in the nearby roadhouse, ice cream salt.

Accruing judgment in hotel bedrooms,
The city of the low escarpment looms,
And for survivors notoriety
Is to have been there. Look behind or burn,
In their good time they marry. If they turn,
It's into Pillars of Society.

Scheherazade in South Dakota

Mitchell (1312 alt.) is situated in the James River Valley and is widely known for its Corn Palace, the only one of its kind in the world. Entirely decorated in corn and products of corn, the exotic-appearing structure was erected in 1921. The Corn Palace each year attracts thousands of visitors from all parts of South Dakota and neighboring states.

Federal Writers' Project. *South Dakota, a guide.*

Implacablest, remotest, levelest!
Immensest prairie, out of what false East

Have you created, dome and corn and spire,
The world of Rimsky-Korsakov entire.

Ill-mated as the nightingale and rose
The brick of Main Street and the *quelque chose*

It partners: all too visible Kitezh,
A Rimsky bauble, bead, and Bangladesh,

Or silent Baghdad of the elder Fairbanks.
Have shops, haphazard banks and doctrinaire banks

Financed it, or (have chickens change of sex?)
Did it their cockerel lay golden eggs.

It is that gleam that to the farm snow-maiden
Poses fresh careers as go-go maiden.

In the small-town still it is a wind
That says "O wondrous land, O land of Ind."

The wind is gone; a whirlwind here and there
Clocks off the dusty time of one more year.

On Sindbad of the store-front time lies heavy.
Rimsky was a young man in the Navy.

46

LORA E. IDE

It's Not Supposed to Be That Way

The river flowed and it was icy and much colder even than the autumn air. And she could see that it was black. And she knew it would be cold.

Already chilled, she stood there in the light rain, there beside the flowing darkness of the river. Her sneakers and socks were wet. She wiggled her toes a little, as she stood there a little hesitantly. They were numb. She shivered. Her sweater was wet, and her jeans were wet, and the oozing, black mud on the bank of the river edged up and over first one sneaker and then the other and still she stood, mere yards but seemingly miles from where she had parked the brown Toyota, there in the dark on the side of the road.

No one passed on the road. All was quiet, except for the rippling and murmuring of the water over rocks, and the swishing of the rain as it hit the leaves of trees around her. She stood listening for the call she didn't hear and wouldn't hear, and when it didn't come she walked closer and closer to the river's edge, finally wading down into it, ankle deep, knee deep, and then waist deep where the river pulled her from her feet with its strength and whirled her away, closing over her head quietly, silently, smoothly in a way that she much appreciated for its lack of fanfare and fuss.

She had a bare instant to think briefly of the times. To think of the rosy college days when that degree had meant something. Those were the days . . . Work hard, they all said. It will pay off. It hadn't. Not for her. Not for . . . him. Meaningless, she thought, gulping cold, black water.

Oh, there had been a brief moment, years and years ago when she had understood the blackness and meaninglessness of life. When that little child she had known, what was his name?, that child, the boy, had been sent, nicely packaged in olive green, to be blown to bits, blown to a trillion bits, in the war. Then, as a child on the sill of womanhood, then she had known. She had been startled out of her youth by the blinding realization that all those bright, pancake Sundays of her past, those Sundays when she and all her siblings had crowded into her parent's big bed warm and squirming like puppies to read the funnies and wait for those delicious fluffy pancakes her mother was making in that warm, sweet-smelling kitchen, were a big fake. Back in those days, when her dad would load his big American station wagon full of plump American kids, both his own and those from next door, and off they'd go to the latest Walt Disney movie, what was it, the Shaggy D.A., or some such movie, back in those days those movies had just seemed like a little extension of real life. But, she found out differently. Yes, sir. Life, real life, was not Disney. She gulped water and choked.

Her own children? How to give them hope, when she knew in her heart that there was none? How to persuade them to work hard . . . in school . . . when it led nowhere? Where to advise them to live, when all around was pollution, cancer, death, defects in the young and innocent coming into a sick, sad world that the powerful and rich were busily making sicker and sadder as fast as they could . . . in order to happily attach another buck. Or so it seemed. Or so it seemed.

And she coughed and gasped in the chilling water and the black all about her closed down over her eyes and her lungs were full of the cold water and thus she died, a 30-year-old victim of the times.

At the funeral they all sat around drinking strong black coffee and eating juicy ham sandwiches on rye with plenty of tasty yellow mustard, and for dessert there were freshly baked chocolate chip cookies.

And it was a gathering of the clan such as had never been seen before, with people who hadn't been seen in 10 years hurrying with alacrity to view the effect those sodden decomposed remains had upon the young husband, such a good man, such a nice man, a hard worker!, and a good father . . . and upon those two golden haired, dewy-eyed children, and upon the rest of the family, so inadvertently left there upon God's good earth.

And she, floating in the pale blue light a little above and to the right of the closed casket, could only remember how the lobster from dinner had made her itch, that gloomy night before she went to the river, and how it had made her sick to her stomach and how she had vomited and had run to the bathroom five times in an hour. Her breasts still itched. At least, the place where her breasts would and should have been. She peered down curiously from where she floated, thinking now of the itching, and then of how nice it was to see . . . her mother, plump and Polish . . . and her mother's mother, plump, gray and Polish . . . and her husband's mother . . . and her husband's grandmother, looking small, gray and wrinkled.

Grammy, she was called. She had always liked Grammy best. Sweet lady. Old. Gray and wrinkled. The small woman, sitting primly amidst the group, suddenly peered up through the blue light with her quick birdlike eyes, spotted her grandson's wife floating there, and winked.

Winked, thought the girl, impossible. But, as she gazed down she saw it again. A wink. Good old Grammy, thought the girl, suddenly warmer than she had been since the river. Always . . . equal to the situation. Irish, thought the girl. Not Polish. Irish.

You can listen if you like, said the voice in her ear. Yes, thought the girl, feeling giddy, I'd like that.

"But she said she was fine in her letters," her mother was saying, clutching the uneaten ham sandwich in her hand, which lay in her lap. "When I asked her she said she was fine, very, very fine, and the last time I called her, she sounded good, and she sounded happy, and I asked her, 'Are you happy?' and she said, 'Yes, momma, oh, yes, momma, I'm happy, so happy, I'm very happy, momma,' and that wasn't so long ago." She then bit into the mashed ham sandwich, and washed the bite down with a dainty sip of black coffee, and then she leaned back exhausted in her chair and her mother, the girl's grandmother, the Polish one, leaned toward her, patting her shoulder, to comfort her.

"You were a good mother, dear, it isn't your fault. There wasn't anything more you could or should have done," said the plump, practical little lady, watching her daughter with concerned eyes.

"Remember," began the older woman again, after a moment's silence, "She was always a little funny. Remember, when she had just finished high school, and her friend . . . died . . . and she, silly child, cried for two solid years? And I told you then, dear, I said, she's funny, and remember, then her uncle died in the river, oh, blessed God, the river," and here the old woman shivered in her turn so that her daughter leaned forward and became the patter, and still shuddering from the thought of her son-in-law, dead these 10 years, the older woman continued, "And I told you then, well, Anna, I

GEORGIA ON MY MIND

said, don't tell her about him, just don't, because remember that little boy, her friend, she reacts so funny to death, and you didn't for a year, a whole year, remember?" Her lovely old brown eyes solemnly sought out her daughter's.

"I remember," replied the dead girl's mother, in a small, sad voice. And the girl, floating there, realized that the pain in her mother's voice had thoroughly chilled her again . . . that watching these two women was both funny and sad at the same time . . . was better, actually, than anything she had seen . . . on television . . . for a long, long time. Perhaps ever, she suddenly thought, realizing at that moment that this was where the black meaninglessness of life dissipated, here in these two women's faces.

She looked away from them and toward her husband. His mother sat next to him, holding his hand. He sat, in stony silence.

Such control, she thought wistfully, as she turned her fading, wavering gaze upon her father. He, poor man, sat between the children, the boy on his right, the girl on his left. She couldn't, no, wouldn't look at the children, though she saw them reflected there in her father's watery blue eyes. And the pain it caused her. And the guilt.

Dad, she gulped, I'm sorry, Dad. I couldn't stand it, I was drinking though it didn't help, and I had no home, nor any love, and no one cared, and I had no money, and no job, and no purpose in dull, repetitious life, except as a mother to those two there beside you, which was enough for many years, for all these years, but . . . when I needed something more, some meaning, it wasn't there, and I had nightmares in the dark, those nuclear things, you know?, and those war things, and those secretary things, and I was lost, and it was all too dark and ugly and that's why I did it, I gave up when it became too much and I decided to just give up and oh, Dad, I do love you and I am so sorry . . . for you.

He turned the blue eyes slowly upward till they found her.

It's okay, honey, he told her. And she, amazed, heard him as if he had said it to her in her ear. It's okay, he said again, smiling at her, showing her with the warmth of his smile that he meant it, it really was okay . . . with him. Wait a bit. I'll be there soon, and then you won't be lonely.

"Why?" she asked him, puzzled.

Because . . . I am old. And, there were things that should have been done. But I didn't do them. It's a mess all right. You are right about that.

There is only so much one man can do, she said to him gently.

Yes, he replied, but I should have tried harder, done something differently.

There are those who should, she replied, tired now, tired to death, and wishing only to sleep.

We all should, he said, with too much certainty to be disputed.

Yes, interrupted Grammy then, Grammy, who had winked. He is right, my dear. In life, one must keep on and on and on. The work is never done, day in and day out, and when one thing that you do doesn't seem quite right, why, then, the next day, you wake up and do it a little differently. That's change. It is healthy. It corrects things.

Life, she went on, is like a river. It goes on and on endlessly. Sometimes it is hard. But you can't stop trying, can't stop working. And, she added, taking a dainty birdlike sip of her coffee, I have learned in my 80 years that it helps . . . to keep your sense of humor.

The river. The girl shuddered as the group faded from her vision and the blue light disappeared and she, poor lost little soul, found herself standing by the river in the wet woods, her clothing soaked, her sneakers filled with mud, her car horn blaring behind her in the dark somewhere.

"You! Hey, You," he was calling. And he turned on her headlights, and he turned on the flash light, and he walked toward her, knowing where she was instinctively, and calling to her, while she said not one word, not a single, solitary word.

He dragged her back toward the car, once he found her, exclaiming over the wetness and the mud and the chill and her general lack of consideration for anybody but herself, and she thought, as he tucked the blanket over her, of the work to be done, and the humor to be delved up from somewhere, and of the blackness and meaninglessness to be rooted out, and she knew the work, the hard work, was before her. What had come before, in her life, was nothing compared to what was still to come.

She would, she thought as she sat shivering there while he drove them angrily home, work hard. She would work hard, she knew, and the way might be lonely, and the rewards nil, but still she would work on and on.

Why? Because . . . decency excluded taking the easy way out. Common decency, it seemed to her, was not so "common" after all. She had learned it from her mother. And some others.

JANE McCLELLAN

Apples to Sell

I have apples to sell,
fine grown apples
that will keep well

        at night
        I write
        baskets of poems

will not rot their cores
beneath deceiving skins

        that I throw away
        in the morning

and because the apples
are something warm
in my hands, because
there is fragrance,
feel of stem, firm
flesh for my thumb;

        poems soggy in damp
        milk cartons, chips
        of cereal obscuring
        the words;

because apples can
compare with other
apples, because
better is a word
grown in an old orchard,

        I have apples to sell:
        I have poems.

A Love Poem from the Pitched Peak of Seventy

I am too old to gild the graying lily
of my head or to crimp its thinning hair
into Shirley Temple curls
(an ivory comb bespeaks my taste
while persuading hair to lie
where none will grow)
but I toss my head in the old
flirtatious way
when he strolls by.

I am too old to shave my legs
or trick them out in ersatz silk
embroidered with a heart to match my own
(and which bleeds more,
a broken heart or
razored shin?)
but I arch my foot in the old
high-stepping way
when he strolls by.

I am too old to smile a coy dimple,
nor could he tell the dimple
from my cheeks' corsage of wrinkles
(pressed roses from Bill or Tom
or Jack or Harry—forgotten valentines
denying love is ever new)
but I simper and purse with all
my gold and porcelain
when he strolls by.

JANE McCLELLAN

I am too old for hot embraces
nor is my breast inflated yet
for pressing close against his chest
(my bra's lace insets
caress a doubled film
of georgette blouse and air)
but when he sits down beside me,
I nibble at his dewlap ear
mousily—as I am not.

ELIZABETH McCANTS DRINNON

Chocolate Candy

The steady, swishing sound of her feet dragging echoed along the tiled floor of the hallway, as she slowly made her way toward the solarium, assisted by the use of a light weight metal walker.

About halfway down the hall she paused to catch her breath and steady herself, backing up to the wall with its handrail to gain a moment of respite. Somehow the hall seemed longer today than yesterday and much longer than last week.

But now she had arrived. "Finally got here, did ya?" Andrew asked, stifling a yawn. He was sitting at a small round table, his three-pronged walking cane standing near his chair.

Ella did not reply. Although she had rounded the corner which led into the solarium, she was still ten feet or so away from the table and a chair. With considerable effort, she struggled through the last stretch and settled herself into a chair which adjoined her husband's.

After she had caught her breath, Ella turned drooping eyes toward Andrew. "Somehow I never thought we'd end up our days in a place like this," she complained. "I would have thought that after raising six younguns, some of 'em would've taken us in when we got sick."

"Now, Ella, you know how much we've been through all that," Andrew said. "Ain't none of 'em got room for us or time to look after us. We decided on our own to come here, remember?"

"No, I don't remember," Ella replied crossly. "I think you made me come. Anyway, that ain't what I come all the way down here to talk about. I want to know how come you've got money to waste on buying chocolate candy for Old Lady Cummins. Never mind how I heard about it—you did buy it from the nursing home store, didn't ya?"

Andrew wiggled in his chair, shifted position, and said, "How'd you hear about it?"

"Never you mind—you ain't got money to be throwing away on nobody, least of all Old Lady Cummins. You know full well that what you get back out of your Social Security check is practically nothing. You ain't got enough to buy your own chewing tobacco and my stockings. Andrew Johnson, I think that the Good Lord

61

didn't give you enough brains to come in out of a shower of rain. You're the sorriest, no account man I've ever seen."

"You're just jealous, that's what you are," Andrew retaliated. "If'n I had boughten you some chocolate candy, old woman, you would've have gobbled it all up. But I didn't buy you none because you're always a-fussing at me."

She looked around sharply and grabbed a half empty bottle of Coke, thrusting it directly into his face. In return, he seized his walking stick and hit her on the shoulder with a sharp blow.

At that moment an attendant of the nursing home, hearing the commotion, came running. "At it again, you two, I see," he said. "I am surprised at you, Mr. Johnson, hitting a woman like that. I am going to have to report you to the administrator and let him decide what to do. You can't hit a woman like that, not at Happyview Nursing Home."

Ella had been listening with growing alarm. "Now, who do you think you are, telling my husband what he can and cannot do, young man? We said our marriage vows long before you were even a twinkle in your father's eyes, and if'n he wants to hit his wife, then that's his business, and not your'n. Now put that in your craw and chaw it for awhile," she asserted.

The attendant stalked off, shaking his head.

Trixie

All night Belle had stood beside an open window, listening to the hooting of an owl in the distance and the far off sound of big trucks changing gears on the highway. All else was still except for the rapid beating of Belle's heart.

Now and then she took a worn flashlight to guide her way to the neatly swept, bare front yard where she stood and called as loudly as she could, "Here, Trixie! Here, Trixie Girl!" But there was never an answering bark from the twelve-year-old fox terrier.

On her periodic trips outside in the darkness, Belle would turn the flashlight's beam on the dirt road in front of the house, weaving the light back and forth in the hopes of catching sight of a small white and brown dog coming home. The flashlight revealed only broom sedge straggling along the road, outlined against fields of young cotton plants.

May blackberries had just ripened, and in the midafternoon Belle had tied on her old straw bonnet, picked up a tin pail, and with Trixie trotting at her heels, had gone up the road a piece to a choice clump of blackberry bushes growing at the edge of the woods.

For an hour or more Belle picked the juicy seeded berries from the low growing bushes, pausing occasionally to pop one of the luscious morsels into her mouth. She was mesmerized by the warmth of the sun on her back and the rhythmic motions of her arms as she reached for the fruit and dropped the berries into the bucket.

Trixie had at first frisked about over the grassy slope, but finally had grown weary and curled up nearby in the shade of one of the bushes to nap. Later when Belle had filled her pail, she straightened, stretched the tired muscles in her back, and turned to call Trixie to go home. The little dog was not in sight, nor was she to be found anywhere. Until darkness arrived, Belle had walked through the surrounding woods, down a path to a small stream, calling, "Trixie, Trixie, here Trixie!"

Finally her husband, John, had joined her rather reluctantly. He, too, called the family pet's name repeatedly, and he took his walking cane to hit at small low growing bushes and brambles. This alarmed Belle even more—did John think that Trixie might be in the undergrowth of briars and brambles, she wondered. If she were there, she would come when she heard them calling, surely, she told herself, unless—that terrible "unless" could not be finished even in her mind, and she refused to consider the possibility that there might be a reason for Trixie's not responding to their searching and calling.

At last complete darkness came rather suddenly the way it does sometimes in spring in Georgia. One moment, twilight had hovered over the countryside, the afterglow of a bright sunset providing sufficient light for their search, and the next moment all light had faded from the sky, and Belle and John could no longer see their hands in front of them.

Tears had begun to stream down Belle's face, and she could no longer withhold her sobs. John turned to her in the darkness and exclaimed, "For God's sake, Belle, shut up. She's just a damned dog after all—not worth sniveling about. Now let's go home. I'm hungry."

Silently Belle had prepared supper for John, warming up black-eyed peas and corn pone, and pouring cool buttermilk from the crock. She could not eat at all. After the meal John had stretched himself and sat down in his favorite chair to read the newspaper. He perused the headlines five minutes, arose, stretched himself again, and said, "Guess I might as well walk around the yard a bit."

Belle could hear him calling softly, "Trixie, here Trixie, here, girl." Presently he came back in and resumed reading his newspaper.

Before John went to bed, Belle made numerous trips outside to call the little fox terrier. She leaned on the gate and remembered the day when Trixie had come to live with them, a tiny pup who had fitted into the palm of her hand, a sassy brown tail curving over her back. Right off, she had acquired the habit of twisting her small body sideways when she greeted Belle and John, the small tail wagging deliriously.

For twelve years she had slept in a half bushel peach basket at the foot of Belle's and John's bed. Sometimes on very cold nights Belle would move the basket to the corner of the fireplace, but Trixie would always whine her unhappiness at the more comfortable location, and Belle would move her back, drawing the woolen rags in the basket closer about the little dog.

During the day when John was working in the field Belle would talk to Trixie. She would tell her about her plans for the day. "I've just got to repot those geraniums on the back steps," she would say, and Trixie would agree that the task could be put off no longer. Or Belle would tell Trixie that "those sweet potatoes just oughter' be dug," and Trixie would wag her understanding. Squinting at the early morning sky, she would ask Trixie what sort of day she thought it would be—maybe hot enough for drying peaches on the barn's tin roof. Trixie, for 12 years, had been Belle's constant companion and closest friend.

Once when Trixie was about a year old, she had become suddenly very listless and weak, and Belle was very alarmed. When John had come in from work at noon, she had insisted that he take a look at the little dog. Without a word, he had gone to splash water on his face out of the bowl on the back porch, and had gone to crank up the old Model-A Ford to take Trixie into town to Doc Dumas, the county veterinarian. The diagnosis was poisoning, and if Trixie had not arrived quickly, she would have died, the veterinarian said. She had gotten into some weed poisoning in the barn. After that, Belle knew that John shared her love for Trixie.

The first rays of light were streaking the eastern sky when John came into the room where Belle was keeping her vigil by the window.

"No sign of her yet?" he asked, rubbing sleep from his eyes.

Belle shook her head wordlessly.

"Ain't no use worrying about her, Belle. She's just a dog, you know. Ain't worth losing no sleep over."

Belle nodded again. "Guess I'll just walk on up toward the black-berry patch to see if'n I see anything of her," he said.

Daylight was coming rapidly and Belle arose to stare out the window up the road, when she saw John striding back toward the house. One of his arms was held curiously straight, and presently she could see that he was carrying something—she dared not breathe—yes, it was something white and brown, but strangely, dreadfully stiff. She screamed.

He deposited the little dog's body on the back steps and came in. "For God's sake, Belle," he almost shouted. "A rattlesnake got her—

that's all. Her head's three times its normal size. Guess she didn't know what hit her—she was way down by the stream. Guess she just wandered off from the blackberry patch."

Belle nodded numbly.

"Just you remember now, Belle, and don't you forget. She ain't nothing but a damned dog," he reminded her.

"I'm a-going to bury her now," he said.

Presently Belle could stand it no longer. It didn't seem right not to be there when Trixie was put away. She went out through the back yard to the rear of the smokehouse where she could hear the steady sound of John's shovel, digging Trixie's grave.

She paused at the corner of the smokehouse and saw John lift the little dog and tenderly wrap her in the old woolen rags from the basket she slept in.

Tears were streaming down his wrinkled cheeks, and as he leaned over to put the little bundle in the earth, his tears sprinkled into the grave. Looking up, his eyes met Belle's.

He said once more, "She ain't nothing but a damned dog, Belle."

ELIZABETH McCANTS DRINNON

Dominecker Chicken Soup

Lizzie raised an arm to pull the worn straw hat down so that her eyes would be shaded from the hot July sun. At the same time she held tightly to the croker sack in her other hand. A loud squawk came from the sack, and she looked down.

"Hush up yo' mouth, you Dominecker chicken," Lizzie admonished. "You's got a good future a-facing you. You's going to make some good chicken soup to help a pretty little gal get well."

The two broiler-sized chickens in the sack were suddenly quiet. Lizzie glanced at the western sky and held up her one free hand toward the sun, moving the width of her hand downward two times toward the horizon.

"Bout two hours by the sun," she judged. "Lizzie, you better be a-hot-footin' it on toward that bus, or you and dem chickens is both goin' to get left."

She moved a little faster now, limping along the winding dirt road with its foot-high weeds growing in the middle between the well worn ruts.

"If'n I had time I would sit down and rest my weary bones a spell," she said, "But old Father Time, he ain't a-waitin' for nobody this here day, not even old Lizzie."

Perspiration streamed down her wrinkled black forehead, ran down her nose and dripped off, but she had no time to waste wiping it off. She wore a white cotton coat, made from flour sacks, bleached and softened from many washings, and her blue and white checked gingham dress came almost to the top of her black high-buttoned shoes.

"Gotta cross that little old branch down there in the bottom," she mumbled to herself. "Good thing the water ain't high—old Lizzie might fall off'n that bridge. Lawsy, I 'member when I could jump across a little stream no wider than that 'un, but can't do it no mo'."

She made her way gingerly across the little bridge and left her footprints in the sandy wet soil near the stream. She glanced once more toward the western sky and rapidly falling sun which was now partially obscured by the tall poplars in the swamp.

Picking up her feet as fast as she could, she rounded a bend in the road and looked ahead. "Jest two mo' turns and Lizzie will be there," she told herself.

Slowly and painfully she made her way, not stopping at all in spite of the ache in her legs and the shortness of her breath. Presently she turned the last bend, and up ahead she could hear the sound of traffic on the highway—trucks changing gears as they ground up the long hill, and automobiles whizzing along. Far in the distance she heard the whistle of the afternoon train.

"Lord, don't let that old bus be gone a-ready," she prayed. "Please, God, don't let it be. You knows that sweet little Rosa Belle needs dese good Dominecker chickens to get her well. Ain't nothing in the whole wide world like Dominecker chicken soup to breaken the big red measles out."

Finally she was at the cross roads and mercifully she found the wooden bench under the chinaberry tree vacant. She put the croker sack down carefully, and one of the chickens squawked in protest.

Lizzie took from her pocket a handkerchief with coins knotted in the corner. She untied the knot and counted out a half dozen small coins.

"Got jest enough for mah bus fare, and a little bit mo'," she chuckled. "And this little bit mo' is a-going to Rosa Belle. Soon's we get dem red measles breaken out, she can buy herself a stick of peppermint candy."

No more than five minutes passed before she saw the old red and white bus come in sight. Lizzie struggled to her feet, gathered up the sack of chickens and raised her arm to signal the bus. It came to a hiccuping stop at the cross roads.

With great effort, Lizzie hoisted herself up the steps onto the bus and handed the driver her fist full of moist coins. "I wants to go to Possum Trot," she told him, just as one of the chickens squawked. "Dat's just beyond Lizard Lope, as if'n you didn't know a-ready."

"Excuse me, Auntie, but what you got in that croker sack?" asked the driver.

"Got me two Domineckers," Lizzie said proudly. "Going to take dem to mah granddaughter who is got a bad case of the big red measles. Ain't nothing like good hot Dominecker chicken soup to make de measles breaken out good. She real sick, she is. If'n de measles don't get breaken out, dey can kill you."

The burly driver scratched his head. "I'm sorry, Auntie. I hate to tell you this, but you can't take no live chickens on this bus. It's against the rules."

Lizzie was dumbfounded and speechless. She stood there in the aisle, debating what to do, still as a mouse.

"Sir, you says I can't take no live chickens on this here bus?"

"That's right, Auntie. I didn't make the rules, and I'm sorry."

Suddenly Lizzie's wrinkled old face lighted up with a bright, toothless smile.

"Just you wait here a minute for me den," Lizzie asked.

She stepped off the bus, went over to the bench under the chinaberry tree and quickly opened her croker sack. She took out a struggling, squawking half-grown chicken and wrung its neck expertly, and then performed the same operation on the other one. Then she put both chickens back in the sack and got back on the bus. The chickens were still flopping desperately.

"Dey ain't live no mo'," she said. "Leastways, dey won't be in another minute or two. Can I go now?"

The driver smiled broadly and said, "Give me your money, Auntie."

Lizzie settled herself down into her seat and put the croker sack at her feet. The warm blood of the chickens had soaked through and it ran onto the floor of the bus.

She looked around, and although no one seemed particularly interested, she repeated, "Ain't nothing like good Dominecker chicken soup to get the big red measles to breaken out."

ROBERT CALDWELL STEWART

Mark me, my pretty Polly

Mark me, my pretty Polly, mark my words:
The crowd is a machine that grinds our joys,
that strips the feathers and the songs from birds,
and the rank ram and eaning ewe destroys.
Mark well the streets its motors waddle in—
the shrieking naked biped there deploys
its mainsprings and its Mafias ad infin.
Come, Polly, bid the city folk good speed.
Tonight we dance upon the lusty mead.

Here upon this cliff

Here
upon this cliff
spray rises
from waves that beat at the base,
and an old wet-feathered eagle soars,
searching for some distant sun.
The ruins there
tumbled upon the top
are covered
with snow, hoarfrost, sleet,
and stones of hail.
I've got the mead, my pretty one—
now where did you say is the warm straw?

The Consolation of King Alfred

Athelney and the dark swamp
The forest and the fox
These my companions
Provide recreation
Offering as they do
Friendship, fellow-feeling, that deep love of kind
And a certain mutual snuffing of the spring wind.
The Vikings have only
Brutality of numbers
Pitiless but reassuring
Like the northern frost
Against a crackling hearth.
We can survive them.

New Year Lines for Sarah Bishop

(Who Lived in a Connecticut Cave from 1797 to 1810)

1

The wind is up. With it the trees yell loud
as if life rushed out of the mouth of death.
And after their parting winter will wrap a shroud
likely, the old whiteshroud, white as this breath,
around him (when the first Elizabeth
reigned, they tell me, shrouds were as white as snow,
white as brides' gowns are now, though then not so).

An animal gets to himself to die;
so the year now, a kind of animal,
will shut us away, not wanting company
here at his death. And for his funeral

72

(after the laying out and shrouding) all
he wishes is the lifted wine, the glass
of greeting once, to say without grief, "this was."

The pigeons in the ivy thrum with the cold,
start echoes muttering in the college gate.
Beyond these walls (new-copied more than old)
the city traffic's tires and horns debate
the right of way. Pigeon and car create
an instant's contrast, but the will of the wind
is master and brings all things to its mind.

2

I wonder was the day a cold one when
they found Sarah Bishop withered to death in her cave
(those puzzled neighbors, honest Ridgefield men
whose wives sent by them what spare food they could save,
might climb West Mountain even with weather to brave);
I wonder too whether she, by death's wind blown,
saw father, sweetheart, God as three, or one?

The spirits of the wind that over her
passed, blessed: Clearly they knew it well—
her father's rage which damped her lover, her
violence and her anguish, till rebel
she must and would and drag, for dogs to smell,
her family's pride through some mean enterprise
which thrust worse than feared shame stark in their eyes.

Then, their humiliation bundled and bound,
God rushed upon her, spinning her mind like a fan.
Pillowed by a stone and bedded on hard ground,
she took cave roof to cover her, never her man.
For thirteen years she prayed and postured, began
to grow into legend, "The Nun of the Mountain, that's
lived out with birds, owls, snakes, stray dogs and cats."

Winter or summer, leaf-fall or leaf-sprouting,
whichever wind blew on that day or night,
she heard of a sudden all the star folk shouting
and dropped her prayers to shatter like her spite
there on stone floor. Her body, grown so light,
seemed white in death and bright as if brand new,
seemed like a leaf the blazing sun looks through.

3

I have no notion why her story starts
out of some images from a winter's day.
I read it first in the papers when my heart's
best fire lay damped, but black banked coals; no way,
except for a red spot here or there, to say
but that it was all out. I had been one
in a tale like Sarah Bishop's, and had run.

Deceit and greed, masked in whatever mask,
ought not be let go by without the lash.
A generous girl, the going price to ask:
So shut up her eyes on the block—"play down cool cash,
call up the Church, ring God, have thunder crash,"
and after fireworks, after religion,
some "hint of social status"—and it's done.

And I, descended from those kings, that rash queen,
ought to have laughed their penny-pride to scorn,
but doubts led doubts. Their sense, though common was keen:
My means to bring the bacon slight; she, born
to some ease and to safety. . . . (I am worn
by great doubt now, reversing in but dreams;
then I had much more cause—and ran, it seems.)

ROBERT CALDWELL STEWART

The Crow

Nescio qua praeter solitum dulcedine laeti
Inter se in foliis strepitant — Virgil

The crow calls to the wanton woods,
barren with winter though they be.
Hail the black bird, may his wayward goods
nurture him as he nurtures me,
and when the long-delaying spring
finds us—as one day it will—
may I to the wanton woods then sing
as he sings wanton to greenwood still.

Crows in Snow

The wind is up and wild today,
shouldering snow in stacks,
the gray garage gone down halfway
beneath these white attacks.

And ninety years expunged and gone
as if they had not been,
but storm to storm were plunging on
in '88 again.

How strange eternity appears
in the storms that frame the lull,
the urgent and conflicted years
stand puzzled, stunned, and dull.

Time is by time now overcome,
but how can it be so
when time is timeless? Here are some
crows perched on stacks of snow.

75

An Epitaph

Crows, perch here.
To me you are dear.
Fox, come to call.
With you I share all.
White winter, appear.
Spring, fetch the green year.
And years, fly away.
Bring the bright day.

The Fox Riddle

I am red with sun   and rust with moon,
with headlights,   two lit coals.
With wind at my will   I wind safe.
The brook then breaks   the breathers who
were once my brothers,   my bothers now.
On roofridge   I recognize
the sign of supper   or sudden breakfast.
Vain singers vie   to avoid me.
They name me never.   You name me.

Connections

At one with fox and flower
my foot goes where it will
in this mysterious hour
and yet is still.

The horror of the bone,
impatience of the blood
stop, like a ringing telephone
that's answered, understood.

But understanding rather
like calling than like thought
has found in fox and flower
this kinship with my foot.

Movements

Pet the dragon on the head
Or be the dragon in his stead.
When the dove did hate the cat,
Wings she lost and whiskers gat.
Ah, with what persistency
We become our enemy.

Javelina T. Hog Woman

She went down to the depot,
'twas Sunday in the dawn.
Her hog was rolling in that day
aboard old Ninety-One.
It was
Javelina T. Hog Woman,
Javelina T. Hog.

It was sent up from south Texas
to the land of ice and snow,
and what she wanted with that hog
was more than God could know.
It was
Javelina T. Hog Woman,
Javelina T. Hog.

She changed her name from Lena
to Javelina T. Hog.
She reckoned to turn meaner
than wildcat or mad dog.
It was
Javelina T. Hog Woman,
Javelina T. Hog.

Her man had run away one day
with a little pink coquette,
but he'd soon have a Lena
that he could not forget.
It was
Javelina T. Hog Woman,
Javelina T. Hog.

She took her prize off Ninety-One,
she reached the town motel,
she flung the door wide open
and shoved in that hog from hell.
It was
Javelina T. Hog Woman,
Javelina T. Hog.

Her man leaped from the bedclothes,
the pink coquette turned blue
when they heard shouted loud and clear
"Have a Lena, you rascal you!"
It was
Javelina T. Hog Woman,
Javelina T. Hog.

The Four-Letter Fad

Great Spavius, forced to prove that he is free,
Must piss for us against a public tree.
Flea-bitten Fido would have passed it by,
But he subserves compulsive destiny.

The Flaw In The Universe Revisited

Two brown rats in a cage
were an experiment.
They were of equal age

and all of the intent
aimed at equality;
but an untoward event

had marred their parity.
One rat had been curtailed
by some dry rot, and he

in tallied glory failed
a final inch or so
of what his fellow trailed.

The sciences may know
something the less for that;
but art can only grow

from nonpareils of rat.
God bless the natural law
for tipping thus its hat

to us who love the flaw,
the seed of things, as well
as what Sir Isaac saw
when that red apple fell.

ROBERT CALDWELL STEWART

The Fable of the Eagle Who Courted a Mouse

The eagle wooed the mouse for mate.
What fine disdain of his bald pate!
Miss Mousie said her worthy kin
Would scoff if one such entered in.
But tell me, Mousie, was it not
The fierce exposure of the spot
Where rocks the eyrie lone and free
That mortified thy kin and thee?

Nature's Old Newness

Out of the four o'clock dark they crew,
those first cocks of the distant dawn.
The moon was up yet, and the dew
dankened the brush it slumbered on.
Among the liveoaks bullbats flew,
but night was gone.

O Nature—with what other name
can we who love you tell our love?
"Goddess" they called you once, but shame
forbids a lover to improve
with false tints his beloved's claim
where truth can move—

O Nature, your fresh ways and times
are flowing through my heart like springs.
Soon birds will greet the morning, rhymes
(like mine) as old as all that sings.
Each new throat with past matins chimes,
and sung day sings.

April

After the exile,
a world-battered Jew
stood, shedding tears of joy in those streets
the enemy had trampled.
And I too
for this long while
stand, struck to the heart by everything that meets
the eye—the unexampled
yellow of the sunbeams where the bright
goblet of that tulip fills with light.

The Spell of Weather

We have been wind-struck and live in a weather spell.
A rainbow played the witch with our heart
until we cannot tell
whether earth is the fallen part
or whether the great gods fell.

Cicadas drone all day in the oaks or sing,
and August hits us hot on the back—
still there's the magic ring.
Sun browns the hay from stack to stack,
as we stand in the spring.

But you, my dear, with the wet wind in your hair
and words whose rainbow shimmers and shades
augur September fair,
when winter (as he must) invades,
will trance the trancer there.

ROBERT CALDWELL STEWART

The Man In The Moon Car

(From *In the Land of Their Exile*)

The oldest memory I have of the moon is not related to the 31st of October at all—or at least it was not so related in the beginning. Strangely, because it is one of those experiences which separate and draw us a little away from the age of technology, it is a memory of an automobile. The experience, which repeated itself many times, comes from the second or third year of my life and from the vicinity of the first house in which I lived, that of my first home, a spot called Wolf's Inn on the edges of San Antonio. My grandmother, my mother's mother, lived with us in those years after my father's death, and often in the summer evenings, barely past dusk when the moon was rising, she would walk with me along the unevenly and blackly macadamised road which ran from our house for half a mile in either direction until it arrived at busier thoroughfares. We would saunter slowly, adopting a pace which was both that of pleasure and that of an elderly, slightly heavy woman who did not need to adjust her gait much in order not to hurry the short steps of a child, and we talked about what we passed. Sometimes it would be the white fox terrier with the brown ear who barked high and quick like a stuffed animal punched in the stomach. Other times it was the lightning bugs darting like little winged flashlights, now among flowers, now across lawns, and now again through the canker grass in the lots which had not been built on yet between the houses. This was the Johnson grass, she told me, and that other (dark green, cool and even) was the carpet grass, and those first had been the cornflowers and the taller ones were larkspur. And then (I held back the knowledge that the words were coming, but was waiting, a little fearful and a great deal joyful, for them to come) she would say, "Oh, Alexander, look, there's that old Moon car." Yes. And it would be there, under the big liveoak tree whose darkening branches cast their shadows out into the moonlit road, shading the car somewhat, bringing a kind of darkness over it, but not obscuring the beautiful shiny (they were always shiny) black fenders in which I could see—in those early days when I could still see well—glinting and glimmering, almost speaking its words of light, the tiny image of the crescent moon.

83

Oh, it was the moon's car—I had no notion at that age that there were manufacturers of cars, least of all one named Moon. Cars were simply raised into being by a call, like the brown-eared dog, like the lightning bugs, like my grandmother and me, like the moon itself. Even after I separated the levels of being slightly and asked one night, "Who drives it, Nan? Who drives that old moon car?" Even after she said, "It belongs to that colored gentleman who calls on the Martinsons' maid." Even then nothing really changed. I saw in my mind's eye a fabulous, fortunate, eternally blessed black man, who drove, night after flying night, the car of the moon, swooped down for a moment from the immortal heavens to our mortal street, and then soared again to his task and pleasure in the cloud-spread kingdom of dusky and gleaming night. No driver has ever replaced that man in the moon's car. In the truest and best nights still he drives her there, and may he drive forever under the wings of the maker of nights through a delight, whatever his earthly fate, like that which he gave unaware to a child who is startled again and finds him wherever a word on a page shined bright by some other poet gleams like a flying crescent from the black fenders of that old Moon car.

JUDY STARLEY VEAL

Carrie's Christmas

The screen door banged shut behind Mary Carrie Flatt as she wandered dreamily out the front door and dropped down onto the steps. The late afternoon sun was warm for December. Carrie's mother had remarked at breakfast that she couldn't remember a Christmas in Georgia ever being this warm. Of course, she didn't mind; but Christmas didn't seem like Christmas without a little nip in the air.

Carrie pushed her dark hair back over her shoulder and turned her attention to the doll in her lap. The doll's pink and white features were a contrast to Carrie's darker ones. "Princess," breathed Carrie as she smoothed the doll's blue satin dress and adjusted her head so the eyes would close.

Around the corner of the porch eight-year-old Elizabeth appeared. Sweat stood out along the bridge of her nose, making the freckles melt. Her red hair was tumbled by the long run up the hill along the path that separated the two roughboard farmhouses.

Elizabeth stopped short when she spied the doll. "How did you get that?" she demanded.

Carrie automatically hugged the doll to her and swung around to face Elizabeth. "I got it for Christmas."

Elizabeth's eyes narrowed as she continued looking at the doll. "You're too old for that doll!"

"I am not. Besides, this is the last doll I'll ever get. Mama told me so."

"It ain't right. It just ain't right for no thirteen-year-old girl to still be getting dolls."

Carrie dropped her eyes and felt the blood rush to her cheeks. "What did you get for Christmas?"

Elizabeth hesitated slightly and declared in her most declaring tone, "I got enough, I'll tell you that!" She reached into her pocket and triumphantly produced a slingshot. Its rough wood had been painstakingly whittled so that little animals decorated the handle. Pride shone in her eyes as she pushed it into Carrie's hand for her to see.

"That's a good one all right," Carrie stated as she inspected the carvings.

When she handed the slingshot back, Elizabeth's eyes fell upon the doll again. "What're you going to do with that doll?" she demanded, her eyes becoming slits again.

"I don't know. Maybe look at her some and then put her in a box in a safe place to keep always." She lowered her voice reverently, "This is the last doll I'll ever have."

"Ha! You don't need that doll. You're too old for dolls," continued Elizabeth as her eyes took in the doll's features and the blue dress.

"Why don't we try out your new slingshot," ventured Carrie as she carefully laid the doll up on the railing that made a shelf around the porch. She looked reassuringly at the doll and then began searching the yard for rocks. Elizabeth's attention was distracted from the doll and she began to collect the rocks, too.

With pockets bulging, they walked around to the back of the house and stopped at the chicken pen. A Coca-Cola crate lay on the ground blocking a hole in the fence. Elizabeth climbed up on the crate and steadied herself by wrapping her toes around the chicken wire. She extracted a small rock from her pocket and tucked it into the pouch of the slingshot. Carrie's eyes were searching the pen for just the right victim.

"There!" breathed Elizabeth as Big Ol' Red came trotting dangerously close to their attack position.

"Knock off his red crown," urged Carrie. Elizabeth pulled back and let go the ammunition. The rock whizzed over the rooster's head and made a ping against the water bucket. Ol' Red walked grandly on by, ignoring them altogether.

"What a rootin' tootin' turkey you are," Elizabeth shouted after Ol' Red.

"AMEN," Carrie responded.

"Brother Ben," shouted Elizabeth, with Carrie joining in to finish the rhyme, "shot a rooster, killed a hen, the hen died, the rooster cried, Brother Ben was satisfied!" They hooted and flapped their arms in mimic of Ol' Red and collapsed on the ground laughing.

"Hey, what you wanna do now?" asked Carrie.

"Let's go see those new pigs Betsy found. Maybe she might be hungry and eat one of 'em right in front of our eyes."

"That's just hogwash!" replied Carrie. "Jimmy Denten told you that so he could make a fool out of you. Pigs don't eat pigs!"

They ambled across the yard and along the path. A thicket of shrubs partially hid the pen from view of the house.

Carrie and Elizabeth drew up close to the fence and leaned over.

"How many did she find!" asked Elizabeth.

"Six," responded Carrie, "but one died."

"Why ? Did she eat it?" asked Elizabeth as her eyes darted for any tell-tale signs around Betsy's mouth.

"No, dummy, it was dead when she found it, and Daddy said he buried it."

"I sure would like to see her eat one," said Elizabeth. She picked up a stick with a leaf on it and leaned over into the pen. "Come on, Betsy, here's a leaf for you." Betsy grunted and continued nursing her litter.

"Carrie!" called a voice from the house.

"Coming," yelled Carrie as she let go the fence and started toward the house. She yelled back over her shoulder to Elizabeth, "If you stand there long enough, maybe she'll eat one."

When Carrie finished the supper dishes, she hurriedly set out breakfast dishes for the following morning. That was a rule her mother had always followed. She had explained to Carrie with pride that that rule was one she had thought of the first week she was married. She expected that she had started a tradition in the Flatt family. Carrie was sure the tradition would die with her mother.

In her eagerness to finish in the kitchen, Carrie broke a cup. She quickly gathered up the pieces in a paper bag and held it over her heart. With eyes squeezed shut she whispered, "Twenty years of bad luck, I bury you with this cup." She plopped it in the trash can and looked up guiltily. Burying it would take so long, and her mind raced to her doll. The decision held. The cup would depart this life in the trash. Carrie giggled and hurried to the porch.

She saw the empty spot where her doll had been at the same time the door slammed behind her. Her stomach squeezed into a knot, and her breath came in labored jerks. Fear crowded behind her eyes as she ran around the house and scanned the back yard. She slowed as she went by the chicken pen, and her eyes took in the empty, chicken-filled area. With even slower steps, she continued on toward the hog pen. Her eyes had taken on a defeated look even before she spied the dirty blue material. The doll was lying near the fence; an arm and leg had been torn from the body. Carrie leaned over and looked into the doll's eyes. She stood without moving for a long time. Then, she reached down and pushed the eyes closed.

A warm, moist, earthy haven prepared and waited for my autumnal entrance.

A rich tangle of green, gold, and crimson foliage entwined themselves among the splendid monuments to nature.

The tree's massive arms held up the sky while the vines snuggled closer, taking advantage of their unguarded strength.

The earth gathered together her earthy odors and impregnated my chamber with her scent.

A snail wound lazily down a fallen, rotted log, oblivious to a persistent butterfly who nipped in and out along his inching trail.

The red and yellow leaves tumbled against one another, vying for the affections of the breeze.

A brown wood spider darted onto my arm, and as quickly left, leaving a thin silvery trail.

The sun looked for me through the winking leaves, and came searching along the green moss.

I held my breath and waited.

The brook tumbled noisily, and gave away my secret place—I relinquished, laughing, and pushed my face up to meet the sun's warm fingers.

JUDY STARLEY VEAL

Winter weaves her greys and browns
And strips the trees
And bleeds the ground
Of life.

And all around are bodies
Like a battlefield
Sunken and grey and sterile—
Termites' food.

And all the green of summer
And rays of sun
Cannot put back life
Where there is none.

———————

A chameleon came and sat
And silently looked round
My pen scratched along the page
As I set my story down.

I stopped my writing and I watched
His chest go in and out
He moved his head from side to side
And rolled his eyes about.

He walked up close and touched my arm
And terror seized him round
He darted down while changing clothes
And went from green to brown.

———————

Storms may rage
Inside my breast
But only contentment
Has known my visage.
My time has gone
I pray that you depart.

The bitter wind
Of a cold april
Has left behind
This wasteland.
An eye can but catch
What the heart already knows.

———————————

When love dies
it does not rot and stink
  like things that live.

It is dead a long time before you can
raise your head
  and catch its scent.

It is a sickening smell, like that of
over-ripe daisies
  that make you nauseous and unable to eat
  and unable to sleep.

Time and silence and wonderful things
do not ease the pain or quiet the heart.
  It is a myth.

———————————

JUDY STARLEY VEAL

I am weary of this wind
That attacks from every side
This man-made beach and the ocean
With its pulchritudinous tide.

I dislike the sticky saltiness
Which the spray leaves behind
And the call of the seagulls
Is lost on a numb and angry mind.

I cannot sit on the windward side
And feel the sun at my back
I can only close my eyes and remember
How you said "This a' that".

And how you looked and how you spoke
And how your hair curled thus
And what it was you said that night
To cause my heart to rush.

If I had known that knowing you
Could cause this great a pain
I'd chart my course o'er emptiness
And stay level with the plain.

I can hear the sounds of your sleep
You, who are filled with self
Your heart is content and full
While fools go sleepless.

It would be good that love go at once
If it must go
Instead of a slip here
And a lie there
While I am watching.

Love's leaving would be bearable
If it were honest
And left boldly through the front door
Rather than the back.

———————

Each year with you
Has been like a day
A short summer day
Exploding with color and scent.

The wild jasmine
And the somber rose
Look and smell the same
Then as now.

And all of time's infiltrates
Cannot change the jasmine
Cannot change the rose
Can only put a blush
On a love that grows.

———————

I have drunk from a goblet of stars;
I have traversed the galaxy and tasted
   forbidden morsels;
I have bathed in the silver drippings of
   the moon,
And I have known the sun intimately.

I have heard the earth cry and shriek
   and tear her green wrappings.
I have seen the sky shed muddy tears
   that stained the oceans.

I have witnessed an omega.

Rough wool pressed against my naked breasts,
   a warm mouth and words
Amid the dying of autumn.
Ugly browns, and dead, rotted wood,
The stench of the earth dying.

In the spring the earth will forget
   the brown,
And wrap a new gown of green around her
   nakedness.

The sun told me she had no soul.

RUTHANNA EWING

Walk A Bitter Road

Scuffing through rough scrub grass to her leaning gate, Rose Crawley looked up at the mid-afternoon sun and cursed. She clutched a big wrinkled grocery bag in one arm. Putting it between her dusty tennis shoes, she mopped at her dripping face with a wadded kleenex. A twisted circle of wire held the gate and to open it she had to unloop this. The gate went down with a jerk into the backed-up earth, and she had to lift it up and over the hump to squeeze through. Then she just stood looking at the shabby grey shingle house. It had nothing to distinguish it from the dozen or so other mill houses up and down the street. If you could call it a street. A lumber yard was within sight, and billows of greyish-white smoke settled over the piles of new boards lying around the low brick building that served as an office. The smell of raw timber and the rasp of saws was constant.

Rose pulled at the bag of groceries. With a grunt, she managed to get it up into her grasp, and heaving it along the railing, pulled her bulk up the split steps of her house.

Through the rusty screen she saw her husband slumped at the kitchen table.

"You George! Come git these damn groceries! I'm havin' a heat stroke. Least ya' could help me in tha' door. Them Rentzes down at the mill store are gonna' steal us blind. You know how much I had to pay for this here stuff? Sixteen dollars an' fifty-eight cents! An' I didn't git but some stinkin' ol' stew beef an' two turkey legs. Didn't have but twenty dollars ta' start with. Looks like Junior could take me to the A an' P once an' awhile."

As she dropped the bag onto the dirty green tablecloth, it split. George laughed, but said nothing. He took a big swallow from the cracked mug he held, then belched loudly.

"Dum' ox." Rose said, lifting her arm to swing at him, then pulled a stool up to the table and poured a jelly glass half full of whiskey for herself. A can of tomatoes and a little can of milk rolled across the dirty worn linoleum. Pushing the eggs and a small loaf of bread aside, she gulped the burning liquid. "Cheap ole' whiskey. You George gonna' die drinkin' this cheap ole' whiskey."

97

But George, eyes now closed, picked up his cup and slowly swirled the drink around. He had a half smile on his face as he reached over to pat her puffy arm.

"Good enuf' fer me, an' ya' don't seem to be minden' it sa' much yer own self."

"An' you know what that Carole Rentz ask me? She tol' me her Billie Joe was gonna' ask our Tessie to the Junior-Senior. An' would we let her go? An' her bein' only fourteen years old an' him bein' at least seventeen. I know he flunked out about two grades, so he's pro'bly a good seventeen an' him only a Junior 'cause he's so dumb."

With each sentence Rose became more agitated. She twisted her frizzy hair into dozens of oily ringlets with two swollen fingers. Then taking a final swallow, began to calm down. The couple sat quietly for the better part of an hour; until the sun sank behind the lumber-yard chimney. Drowsing, they heard a car door slam, and voices outside. Rose moved unsteadily from her stool. She leaned down to try to gather the scattered groceries. Shaking George, she hissed, "Git on in the other room, you old drunk fool! Tessie's a-comin' an' you know how she hates ta' see us jus' sittin' here."

She grabbed at the near empty bottle and lurched over to a chest in the corner. Shoving it back behind some wadded towels, she turned just in time to greet her frail looking daughter. "Tessie—you sure late tonight. You have practice?" Then glancing out the door, she saw a truck. It cranked up as Rose shouted, "Who that bring you home? That Rentz boy? That no-good dum' ox. Why in tha' world his mama thinks him so special, is beyond me. You're not to ride out with him no more, you hear? You're never to git in his ole' rattle-trap truck agin' or even talk to him agin' ever. You hear me now, Tessie? I'll take the strap ta' your backside. I mean that! I ken yank those blonde curls outta' your head, missy!"

Hands on her hips, Rose watched Tessie slowly pour a half glass of milk from the bottle still on the table. Then pushing past her mother with scarcely a glance, she went down the hall to her room. Rose sat at the table again. What in the world could be wrong with the child? Sompin' bad was eatin' at Tessie. Or mebbe' it was that Billie Joe Rentz. God in heaven! What if that Billie Joe had got her in trouble, an' they had to' git married? Course her and George had ta' hurry up things a little counta' Junior, but in them days it was different. Somehow she wanted more for Tessie.

Rose had gone through many a bad time with George, but she guessed he was about as good as she coulda' got. If only he wouldn't drink so much—an' git out an' find him a job. Junior said he might git him back on at the mill, parttime. But George was always feeling so bad, he couldn't git hisself together ta' go see about nothin'. If she had a job, she might could send Tessie ta' Business School. If George didn't git better they'd be comin' for the house, purty soon.

The same old ideas kept circling through Rose's mind. Trying to untangle them was as useless as trying to make George quit drinking—or herself, for that matter. Tears rolled from her squinty eyes and she let them drip into the cracked green oilcloth, fascinated at the pool they soon made. If only them Rentzes had never came ta' run the mill store. They blamed her dog fer tearin' down tha' fence. An' one time they called the cops when her and George was jus' foolin' around. Shucks—her an' George used ta' always be foolin' around at each other. But no more. An' they was never no louder'n most of tha' other people that lived on that street!

She began to think how she'd like ta' throw one of these eggs at ole' Coralee Rentz. That made her think about bein' hungry. She ripped open the loaf of bread and stuffed two slices into her mouth. Chewing noisily, she gulped at a can of diet cola, left open on the table. It had long since gone flat but she finished it, then got up to start supper. She'd better sober George up. Hardly any need 'cause he'd jus' go ta' bed anyhow. Or let tha' ol' goat lay where he was all night! Bed alone felt good, anyhow. George had been a humdinger in his day, but he sure was sorrier' n' a cold fried egg these times. No matter.

Rose put a boiler of water on the old burner to cook the potatoes. Peeling them, she pared off huge chunks and stuffed them into her mouth. Then she chopped up carrots. Twisting the top, she threw it at a scraggy dog that wandered into the kitchen through the half-open screen.

She heard Junior clumping up the steps. Wiping her hands, she turned. He shoved his lunch pail across the table and began to unbutton his workshirt. Taking it off, he wadded it into a ball and threw it at his mother playfully. "Hey, old lady. How's the Beauty Queen of 1900?"

Rose picked it up and folded it. She reached out to give her huge son a kiss. "Big ol' bear! Oh you ol' Junior. Teasin' your mama like that. Supper's ready but ya' better see how about Tessie. She's cryin' agin'."

Then, "This fryin' stew meat is stringier than ole' Coralee Rentz' neck, but Junior, I had ta' go to the mill store 'cause ya' didn' ever take me to tha' A an' P. Your dad didn't do a thing agin' today, Junior. What we goin' do, Junior? What you reckon we better do?" Junior was gone.

While the vegetables boiled, Rose tried to count backwards in her mind. But Tessie's plight was too complicated for her non-mathematical mind. Heaping a plate, she stirred greasy meat with a thick gravy and poured it over all. "C'mon, Junior. I'm eatin'. You an' Tessie c'mon."

Junior returned to the kitchen and fixed his own meal from the pots on the stove. He pulled out the stool and sat opposite Rose, then rose to bring the gravy skillet to the table, to pour over slices of bread.

Rose watched her big son. She could tell how much he enjoyed her efforts. "I put some tea in that there jar over there, son. Wan' me ta' git it for ya?" She ruffed his wet hair as she went past him, and ran her hand across his broad shoulder. 'Law, how she loved that boy!' When she set his tea beside his plate, she resumed her own meal. Then, "What's wrong with Tessie? She comin' ta' eat?"

"Said she wasn't hungry. She'll git sompin' when she gits back."

"Gits back? Where's she goin? If she's out with that Rentz no-good agin' tonight, I'm gonna' switch her, sure enuf'."

"Billie Joe ain't that bad, Mom. He's sure liken' Tessie."

"Huh. He kin like her all he wants. But he better stay away from her. You reckon he got your sister in the family way, Junior?" Junior pushed his plate back. He finished the last of his tea and stood up, ignoring his mother's question.

"I'm goin' to wake dad up and make him eat sompin'. He's gettin' worse and worse, Mom. Looks like you could git him to switch to beer some of tha' time! Mebbe' we should take him to see Dr. Steele sometime. I could take him Saturday."

Rose heard George give a groan as Junior moved him. "Come on, old goofer, ya' gotta' eat now. Wake up, Dad." Then "Mom, come in here. Dad's actin' funny. He been drinkin' all day without eatin'?"

Rose struggled to her feet. She looked into the other room. George lay half off the couch. His face showed grey and contorted, even in the half light from the old lamp. His eyes were closed. Head back and mouth gaping, he was making gutteral noises with each breath.

Rose pulled him up onto the sofa and sitting on its sagging side, put her ear down his chest. "He sure is a breathin' bad, Junior. Oh my God. He must be dyin'. Call Tessie. That's a dyin' rattle sure nuf'. Tessie. Your dad's a 'goin'. What'll we do, Junior?"

Rose, now crying hysterically, started to pound on the sick man's chest. Tessie, hearing the commotion, came out of her room. When she saw her father in such a position, she tried to pull her mother away. "Mom, he's got to breathe. Let him alone." The girl tied her robe around herself as Billie Joe and Junior rushed to the couch and started to lift the man.

"Oh no ya' don't, Billie Joe Rentz. You ain't touchin' my George, as sick as he is."

"Shut up, Mom. We gotta' git dad to Dr. Steele's. Billie Joe's out there with his truck, n' says he'll take us. If you want ta' come, come on. But iffen' ya' don't, stay here. You an' Tessie. He's bad though, that's for sure."

The two boys lifted George and half-dragging, carried him down the steps to the truck. Tessie ran out and jumped into the back, pulling him up and onto her lap. She carefully pulled a blanket over him.

Screaming obscenities at all three, Rose watched them drive away. Slamming the screen door, she kicked out at the dog. "They kin' all go ta' hell for all I care."

She didn't know how much later they came back. With her arms around the empty whiskey bottle, she was asleep. Junior came into the room and touched his mother's arm. She roused, then sat upright. "You been gone long enuf'. Most two o'clock. Where's Tessie? How's your dad?"

Junior sat down at his father's place and said bluntly, "Dead. He was dead when we got there."

"Dead! That George dead? He can't be!" A shudder ran through Rose. She sat staring past Junior vacantly—out the door at Tessie, who cried quietly on the porch. Billie Joe's arm was around her. Then, as if the fact had finally penetrated her brain, "Tessie, you done hear your father dead, an' you jus' standin' there with that boy? You git outta' here, boy! An you Tessie git in here, an' do yer' grievin'. We'll have to be makin' plans. What we gonna' do, Junior? You the man of the house now, I guess. Poor ole' George musta' been sickern' I thought. Never shoulda' let that Rentz boy take him to the doctor in that ole' rattly-trap truck a' his! If only I da' knowed. He done shook my George ta' death."

As an afterthought, "Wonder if that there insurance money'll take care tha' funeral?"

Tessie made no move to come into the house. Rose pushed the screen door out with a kick. Grabbing the girl's arm, she heaved her into the kitchen. Then she rushed out to yell at Billie Joe. "You no-good sorry Billie Joe—git off this porch an' leave us ta' our private grievin'. An' you kin' tell your mom, ole' Coralee Rentz, we don' want none of *her* sympathy, neither! You hear?"

ZACK HOKE CARTER

Miz Faust's Concert A Grand Slammer

Dateline May 12th—"Tornadorish," "pert," "cracklin," "determined" were exclamations heard from the 150 some-odd folks in the Trout Warre Music Hall of Mercer Institute for the Advancement of Percussion Instruments. They were assigned to the piano-playing of Miz Sarai Fowst, who attacked the keyboard with a vigor comparable to Uncle Buddy's billygoat charging Oscar Boone's dime store. So far as I am concerned, every one of her pinkies is deserving of the Black Belt of Karate fame and distinction. Speaking about "determined," Professor Daniel Dufy Defore was said to have remarked that the jutting chin, the tongue and underlip motion, and the swingin loose hair of Miz Faust made Mr. Albert Durer's *Knight* look like a wishy-washy Mr. Milquetoast.

After a fast warmup of soft vulgarian Bartok melodies, she galloped on with Mr. Galuppi's famous and well-known sonata. The presto con fuoco shook and rumbled like July thunder roarin down Peanut Valley toward the Terrell County courthouse. Next she buzzed through Mr. Lud. Beethoven's f-minor Op. like Junior Ryal's Poulan chainsaw wreakin havoc on a 24 inch pine tree. Buck Acree even admitted that at close range he felt invisible woodchipnotes, as it were, banging into his face, so explosive was the effect.

After the smoking-tobacco pause, she really got wound up. Nothing can describe her back-wrenchin, head-flickin, tongue-twistin, teeth-grittin feat any better than the way Coach Will Mabry used to talk about that square-jawed fullback of the Valdosta Injuns when he had his dander up: "Indeed, indeed, he is certainly full of piss and vinegar." One might even go on to say that "chopsticks" could apply not only to them things the Chinese eat with but also to the meat cleaver technique of the artiste's delicate hands. By godfrey, think of chopping Chopin with chop-sticks! And it come out good. On the c-sharp minor Op. I counted twice when she hit five notes faster than an active woodpecker's draw-back.

For the extra piece, following much clapping and approving nods, Miz Fawst selected a lovely tune based on the rowdy Punch and Judy puppet shows of merry ole England. Time running out meant that she ended rather abruptly, leaving the audience in mid-breath, sucking in. The entire performance left this reviewer with perpetual-motion chill bumps crawling swiftly up and down the spine, a phenomenon not felt with such intensity since last I visited Mable's Musical Muscle Massage Parlor in Vidalia, which is about as big a compliment one could expect from a man like myself. A good time was had by all, and those I talked to said they hoped this yankee Miz would come back again to visit with us.

#30

Zack Hoke Carter, Music Critic
Macon Democratic Inquirer

CYNTHIA ADAMS

An Autumnal Entreaty

Do I die, too,
As Autumn comes,
To rouge the green,
Her colors to claim?
Do I die, too?

Do I die, too,
As Autumn leaves,
As she takes her hues
   to another place,
   far away?
Do I die, too?

O Autumn, gypsy that I am,
Could I but go with you,
   rather than to stay,
To look at that gray sky,
Trees etched against the
   pewter day?
O, take me with you!
Don't make me stay!

DAVID HIGHTOWER

Southern Snow

The southern night
　　turns an astonished white
As unexpected snow falls
　　covering this unaccustomed land with white,
Tracing the dark of outlined trees
　　that weave a design of black cracks
　　　　against this pale vision.
All grows to sudden silence
　　except the muffled steps
　　　　of the awakened . . . curious,
Drawn to explore this new world
　　with hesitant steps and lowered voices,
　　　　awed by the beauty of this flake built temple.
It is a holy magic to snow starved eyes,
　　and a memory is already growing:
　　　　soft touch of falling flakes,
　　　　　　breath of crystal in the night,
　　　　cool wonder of steps softly cushioned,
　　　　　　and the still stopping of all time
　　　　among the breathless trees.
It makes the world more real,
　　even more than real;
A tale to tell the unbelieving summer sun,
　　who will scoff and say,
"That's just a dream that you once dreamed
　　trying to fool that sweat running down your body."

Old House

There is something familiar,
　　something strange and sad
About this old house
　　long abandoned,
Forgotten and incredibly gray,
　　almost shimmering among the mysterious,
　　　silent whisper of pines.
The sagging, sunbleached porch
　　grins crookedly
　　　into the clear, unblinking eye of the well,
As they listen to the decayed flowerbed's dream
　　of some wrinkled grandmother's lifegiving hands,
Creating yellows and blues among the weeds,
　　and weaving this tangle of rose bushes,
That dance triumphantly red
　　into the white heat of noon.

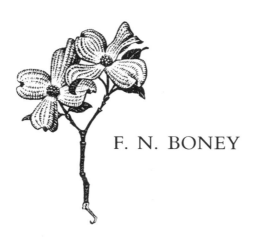

F. N. BONEY

The Redneck

The redneck—that is, by national definition, the Southern white workingman—is rapidly emerging as one of the most distinctive, disgusting characters of our time. Hippies, imperialists, effete snobs, Black Panthers, flunkeys of the Establishment, Mafia mobsters—none has the force and focus of the infamous redneck, the pale beast of Dixie who stalks Negroes, Yankees, Federal officials, United Nations representatives, and all the other good guys. He looms large on stage, screen, radio, and television, and he dominates many newspaper stories, magazine articles, and books, especially some recent genres of the modern novel. His beefy, bestial image is deeply embedded in the national mind, and even his scrawny, savage women and sallow, vicious children are gradually finding a place in the American nightmare. He is the last dregs of our sick society, the ultimate bottom of the barrel.

In an age when any kind of profanity and slander goes, when an old fighting phrase like "son of a bitch" has become almost a term of endearment, when Oedipus apparently lives again in every man, even the thickest white skin can still be penetrated by the terrible epithet "redneck!" This white equivalent of "nigger" really stings. And why not? This one word, two syllable slander is devastatingly thorough. It not only shatters the immediate victim but also degrades his ancestors and damns his descendents. Like its granddaddy, "poor white trash," it reaches to the very genes, a modern curse of Cain.

Viewed from a distance, the South's damned white proletariat, undereducated and oversexed, seems to have been disastrously prolific (but just because the Lord made so many of them doesn't mean He loves them; God is a tasteful person). There are just too many rednecks; so, for the convenience of a clear image, certain groups within the larger class are emphasized. Nasty law enforcement officials, forlorn tenant farmers, select "linthead" factory hands, and a mixed bag of unemployed rural thugs populate the image of the redneck, but, narrowing the focus even more, one basic type emerges as evil incarnate, the service station attendant.

115

Here at last in the midst of an imprecise, fluid era is an undiluted, unchanging villain, the Aryan storm trooper who lurks in every grease pit south of Cincinnati and east of Dallas. He is the perfect bad guy for a people desperately in search of personified sin. Even the swiftest, most superficial traveler through Dixie can recognize this creature's dark (evil, that is) nature. Everyone knows what his soft accent and accommodating manners really mean; even the naivest tourist can stop the belligerence seething just beneath the surface. No amount of amiability can conceal the hair-trigger hatred ready to lash out at the slightest pretext. Certainly anyone with even a passing acquaintance with Truth (a couple of "relevant" college courses) can recognize the redneck for just what he is, a racist beast.

Yet there are always a stubborn few who refuse to accept the evidence of their senses and their souls, who somehow remain uncertain of their ability to analyze instantly Southern auto mechanics individually and the Southern white proletariat in mass. Fortunately for these reluctant Jeremiahs, help is available from a small band of highly specialized Southern liberals who will tell all—for a fee. These self-proclaimed heroes of the great Southern morality play are often expatriates residing in New York, Chicago, or some other Beulah land of modern America, including a number of college campuses. But wherever they come from and wherever they are now, the story is much the same—a stirring autobiographical odyssey up from knavery. This particular type of Southern liberal is often himself kith and kin of the rednecks, sometimes less than a generation removed from the pale rabble. This bothers him, really obsesses him, and in order to be cleansed forever of this terrible taint he repudiates his lowly cousins with an intellectual and moral passion seldom matched even by Southern patricians in their periodic denunciations of "lesser breeds" of Southern whites.

But whatever their shortcomings, these Southern liberals perform a splendid service for their troubled country. Their attacks on rednecks not only boost their own egos (and incomes) but also strengthen the morale of a nation rapidly losing confidence in itself. Their message may be the psychological salvation of the American people who, faced with a host of frustrations and failures, can console themselves with the thought that no matter how deplorable things seem to be getting, conditions have to be much worse in the land of the white niggers. Every real (non-Southern) American knows that however much he blunders or degenerates he will remain superior to the vile redneck, the nation's last, best mudsill. And besides, what true American could help being inspired by the spectacle of a confession of sin, especially Southern sin, and a profitable business transaction being performed simultaneously—a kind of moral double feature.

These "I was there" testimonials by prophets not without bile in any country are further reinforced by the voluminous contributions of non-Southern scholars and experts who have tarried long enough in Dixie to confirm what they knew in the first place. These intellectual sons of New England are, of course, as impartial and unbiased as ever, and they retain enough of the ancient Calvinism to remember a cardinal theme of the national creed—the depravity of poor white Southerners, the unelect. Most of these learned fellows travel fast and light through the Southern provinces, often carrying only typewriter, camera and/or tape recorder, and a medium-sized suitcase which strongly resembles the lengendary carpetbag. They hit all the low spots, generally stopping only at massacre and atrocity centers, occasionally examining the region's moral degeneracy firsthand, anything for the sake of social science (and royalties).

They see all the auto mechanics and other rednecks necessary to confirm the grimmest stereotypes. These busy scholars are, in a morbid sense, fascinated by the animal antics of the direct descendents of seventeenth-century Europe's poor white immigrants, especially in contrast to the dignified behavior of Mother Africa's children. Rednecks wolf down coarse, greasy food; blacks, partaking of the same fare in a similar manner, simply consume soul food. Some rednecks guzzle moonshine whiskey and carouse through the night, but any black behaving in a similar manner is simply demonstrating a unique life-style. Any poor white driving a big, new automobile is a spendthrift; a poor black in the same vehicle is an innocent victim of our consumer culture. Intellectually, rednecks are hopelessly backward; similar blacks are educationally deprived. And so it goes. Caught in the same act, the redneck can do no right, the black no wrong. Obviously, every scientific measure points to the redneck as a regional and national albatross, a curse on the land from the very beginning.

Thus the complete picture emerges, ugly but eloquent. Some bad seed were planted in the English colonies south of Pennsylvania at the very dawn of European colonization, and this pale, prolific strain of humanity has repeatedly besmirched American civilization as it unfolded over more than three centuries. The American dream, man's last, best hope, still occasionally blossoms forth in a Hoboken here or a Gary there, but, due in no small part to the pernicious influence of the redneck, it can never reach its full potential— Paradise never quite won.

The whole story, a good old-fashioned Yankee camp meeting epic, is complete and lacks only one ingredient, accuracy. Who are the rednecks? What are they really like? In many ways rednecks are typical Americans with typical American attitudes. They as much as any group in our culture are representative Americans. This is a simple fact and not nearly as sad or shocking as it first sounds. Working class Southern whites are, overall, decent sturdy folk with more virtues and less vices than advertised. Viewed unemotionally and rationally, they compare favorably with many of their critics.

This is the truth of the matter, a very hard truth that most Americans have never been able to accept. Rednecks are neither stupid nor lazy; their lack of overwhelming affluence is primarily caused by environment, not heredity. They are not well educated either, but again environment is the main explanation. Like many other adults who had to go to work at an early age, rednecks often are anxious for their children to have a better chance in the academic world, and some are self-taught to a surprising degree. Rednecks are not without ambition and drive; for generations they have fed the swelling ranks of the middle class with a steady stream of economic immigrants. But often they are more aware of the price of success than many of their "betters." They are less greedy and hence more gracious than most. Yes, the redneck has manners, or, to put it in more "meaningful" terms, a kind of live-and-let-live concern for the feelings of others, a "do your own thing" sort of toleration much proclaimed but little practiced by the "now" generation. This is a precious asset in an abrasive civilization, a culture whose social machinery is gradually breaking down due in part to a shortage of just this kind of personal lubrication which allows dissimilar people to coexist with some degree of harmony. How incredible that the plain redneck with his rough but real manners might possess a remedy for some of our social ills. The gentle, mild hypocrisy of formal politeness, always strong in the naive, old South, just could be very good medicine for our snarling society.

Like everyone else, the redneck wants to share in the material benefits of American life, but he retains some restraint and even dignity in his pursuit of this goal. Often he has a finer sense of value than many of his contemporaries. A quiet day fishing with his sons, a night out with the family at the drive-in theater or the ball park, and many other "hick" activities involving primarily a man, his wife, and his children—these increasingly outdated diversions from the normal work routine are more and more valuable in a culture where the family is rapidly disintegrating and many children, especially privileged children, grow up empty and belligerent and thoroughly confused. The growing number of rootless, restless, potentially hysterical youngsters groping through the nation's schools and universities is evidence of the high cost of our materialistic, modern way of life. The redneck culture looks more attractive every desperate, destructive day.

Most rednecks treausre their family and their friends and retain a sense of integrity—even honor—in an increasingly crass, corrupt age. Many are men of their word at a time when many men's words mean nothing. They are open and direct in a devious milieu. They can be quite naive and sentimental and even foolish, but these tendencies hardly set them apart from other Americans. Rednecks are as American as Rap Brown's proverbial cherry pie. Condemn them if you will, but do not forget to apply the same critical standards to other Americans with equal vigor.

But what of racism and violence, other bits of Rap Brown's America? Alas, the redneck is a racist, at heart believing that blacks are different and inferior, but how could he believe otherwise in white America. The redneck did not invent racism, and he certainly has no monopoly on it now. White Americans, North and South, prosperous and poor, have always been contemptuous of "lesser breeds" of every size, shape, and color. From Pequot Indians to Asian peasants, from the beginning to the present, white Americans have always looked down upon their little black, brown, and yellow nonbrothers; white racism has always been a central theme of American history. The redneck has only been more candid than most in expressing his All-American racial attitudes.

Actually, when it comes to head-on, hard-nosed racial hatred, the redneck is sometimes a little remiss by national standards. He has lived among black people for generations; for centuries the destinies of the white and black folk of Dixie have been closely intertwined, inextricably blended into what is sometimes called the Southern way of life. Southern whites, especially rednecks, have coexisted with blacks under almost every conceivable human condition, usually living in a rough, unequal, peculiar kind of harmony, but sometimes fighting and occasionally loving. Physical and psychological blending has occurred, far too much for either group to ever realistically believe in totally separate cultures, but at the same time the bloody, brutal chapters of the story are remembered by both groups. Finally reacting, indeed overreacting, to traditional white racism, many blacks all over the nation are developing their own brand of ethnic vanity, a new variation in old American racism which gains strength at the very time some older white forms of the same basic insanity appeared to be fading slowly.

This dark, new racism is a dangerous temptation for bitter, frustrated black people but a real godsend for many white liberals who have always preferred a long-distance sort of arrangement with their black brothers—at least across town or, better still, something like the distance between Westport, Connecticut, and Selma, Alabama. The vocal university professor who champions integration of the public schools need no longer rationalize tucking his own children away in a racially sanitized private academy. The bright-eyed nun who never misses a civil rights demonstration can stop pretending that the parochial school she teaches in is truly integrated. The public-spirited businessman who champions fair employment practices can stop ignoring the racial and religious restrictions at his golf club. Pert, young housewives will no longer have to slip quietly back to lily-white suburbia (and their stray families) after working all day to save the ghetto folk. For these people black pride is beautiful. What used to seem more than a wee bit hypocritical is now wholly progressive. The kind of racial separatism the redneck is condemned for defending in the rural South can now be openly, even proudly

120

rather than quietly practiced by liberals who will no longer be challenged for simultaneously championing and avoiding the black masses.

Black militancy is even more attractive to the revolutionary radical who really desires to destroy contemporary society. Terror and violence will be necessary, and young militant blacks will make splendid cannon fodder when "Der Tag" arrives. This kind of cold-blooded manipulation of the black masses would shock the cruelest of rednecks, but the real zealot, convinced of his own rebel righteousness, knows that American society (like some Vietnamese towns) must be destroyed to be saved. Black or white bloodshed along the rapid road to salvation is purely incidental. More moderate radicals who really only seek significant reform are also playing a dangerous game with the black militants. Whatever temporary advantages are gained by encouraging Negroes to become more active and more isolated will not compensate for the ultimate risk—indeed, near certainty—of permanent estrangement. A few reforms won by pressure and confrontation will be worthless if black-imposed racial segregation evolves in the process. Better to challenge a few black fanatics now—to cancel their special privileges and evaluate them just like rednecks and other ordinary people—than to try to coax their followers out of armed enclaves later.

Racism, white or black style, usually flows from emotional rather than intellectual sources, but, again, under close scrutiny, the redneck often pumps less adrenalin under pressure than many of his cultural superiors. Indeed, the centers of frenzy in contemporary life are not Southern service stations and general stores but the nation's institutions of higher learning where a growing minority of students and professors have discovered ultimate truth and lost interest in the free interplay of intellects and ideas. This academic emotionalism has greatly reinforced the black power movement, a crusade few dare question at many of our most famous universities. Though not as public, emotionalism is hardly absent in the established spheres of business and government either. Incredible as it may sound, the time may have come when controversial problems are as sensibly examined by Southern redneck grand juries as by the ubiquitous blue-ribbon committees loaded with distinguished educators, statesmen, and industrialists. The redneck has not suddenly become wise, but the elite seems to have become foolish.

But even fools recognize the danger for emotional racism. Upper class Americans shudder as they witness unruly rednecks—or, almost as nasty, Northern workers—resisting large-scale integration on the evening television news. They are still outraged the next morning when they drive their own children to school—past several grimy public schools and on to a safe, sheltered private or parochial institution. Such educational refuges are not available to the children of rednecks who, along with their black classmates, must bear the main responsibilies of a social experiment vocally championed by the elite establishment. But, of course, it is ridiculous to expect the elite to commit their children to such earthy, flesh-and-blood reform. It would make as much sense to expect the Kennedys, Johnsons, Nixons, and other national leaders of our democratic society to enroll their children in the District of Columbia's public schools. Some things are just not done by the better classes in the land of the free.

Place middle and upper class Americans in the same social squeeze now being experienced by many lower class whites, especially but not exclusively rednecks, and then passionate response would be much greater. The redneck is often too moderate and decent for his own good. He is a relatively nice guy in an increasingly nasty age, and so he is simultaneously ridiculed and exploited by his "betters." His considerable respect for tradition and compromise (distant relative of law and order) keep him largely in line for the present, but he is a man who has never been afraid of a fight, and precise patterns of disruption and violence have been demonstrated by other groups in contemporary society. Through the magic of television he has gotten the message—anything goes in a good cause.

And, of course, violence has been a part of the redneck's heritage, but, as with racism, how could he escape it? From the beginning American culture has condoned force and violence. From knife and tomahawk through cannon and atomic bomb America has always been a violent land, and the redneck has certainly contributed his share to the general mayhem. For that matter, so has the black man. Some scholars have described this excessive violence as primarily a Southern phenomenon, a unique regional blood-lust binding rich and poor, black and white in a kind of kamikaze culture. This viewpoint is reinforced with selective statistics and partisan insights to reassure the rest of the nation. The lynch mob is often presented as a good example of Southern decadence—whoever heard of a Western lynching or a Northern mob? In reality neither the redneck in particular nor Southerners in general have ever had a corner on violence, a national characteristic. Under the proper pressure all Americans lash out in blind, deadly rage.

In a broad context the settling of a wilderness continent required force and violence. Historically violence was an asset and a necessity in the formative stages of the United States. The lowly redneck, tough and tenacious, made a major contribution in this long struggle for survival and conquest. In dozens of battles and numberless skirmishes he drove back the red men of the forests and plains, and he was in the forefront of the armies that fought Britishers and Mexicans and, more recently, more alien people in distant lands. There is no shortage of rednecks in the neat, quiet American military cemeteries which now dot the globe. However rejected in normal times, the redneck has always been welcomed when the nation went to war.

Appropriately enough, the redneck's finest fighting hour came when the Old South became the wartime Confederacy, a truly lost cause. But even in defeat the Confederate soldier won a peculiar kind of honor. A nation which worships success still, almost in spite of itself, looks back with admiration at the Johnny Rebs who failed. The appeal of the Confederacy is a complex phenomenon which includes unwholesome elements, but primarily it is based on the fighting power of the rebel army which in turn was primarily based on the redneck infantry. Poorly clothed and inadequately equipped, the plain redneck—better known then as the "yeoman farmer"— fought with great dash and determination long after many of the vaunted aristocrats began to waver, and, even more suprising, he came within an ace of defeating a vastly superior enemy.

Under vastly different circumstances he fights on today in another lost cause. Together with his black comrades-in-arms he is the cutting edge of the American army assigned an impossible combat mission in Southeast Asia. As usual it is a rich man's war but a poor man's fight. The redneck is doing the fighting and dying, but he is certainly not responsible for this debacle. There is blame enough to spread widely, but fundamentally the responsibility rests with the privileged classes—yes, the establishment. The redneck did not seek this war. It evolved from the combined wisdom of some of the most admired members of our contemporary aristocrat—a Dulles, a Rusk, a Bundy, a Rostow, a Lodge, a Johnson, a Taylor, a Kennedy (or two or three), a Bunker, and on and on through the higher echelons of business, education, and government. The redneck is certainly not the villain nor can the South be isolated for special condemnation. Actually a strong case could be made for the primary responsibility of proud, old New England, but a search for scapegoats will not solve our current problems. To achieve real, lasting reform, the American people will have to stop looking for personal culprits like rednecks (or blacks or Communists or Jews or hippies of even members of the Establishment) and take a much broader, deeper look at our way of life. A good way to begin this new approach is to stop blindly berating the poor redneck. After all, he is, in his own idiom, "a pretty good old boy."

PEG SIMMS

I Dream of Ancestors

They hacked enormous stones
And set them square.
They heaved great timbers under me
And spread them out like dark streets.
They laid naked trees above me
To barricade the sky
And sling the rain away like whips.

They spun sand as smooth as skin
To line the walls;
Fired it to dazzle me with light
And halt the wind.

They placed the house
With its back to storms,
Opened its arms to sunlight,
Planted it on rock.
No violence breaks it.

They put God in temples
As simple as barns and as honest.
Like prophets, they struck ground
And water flowed.

They raised rebellious flags
Under the wide eye of God.
They murdered in long battles;
Were murdered.
They fell like giants.

They rose in vast acres of sorrow.

They tore open the earth.
Like discus throwers, they hurled mighty seeds
Out of sight,
Caused a riot of crops, doomed.
Then they threw themselves down in rows,
Dragged granite over their faces,
Named themselves.

They are not stilled.
From the roots of strong vines
They speak to me.
They whisper blossoms.

Behind a mass of ancient trees,
Renewing with fierce green,
As they were told to do in the
        beginning,
I lie beside high windows.

I am like a dead queen,
Biered on an old bed,
Held aloft and horizontal for all to see.

I am hollow as bones,
As transient as dust.
I withered in song.
My pavane was played by sweet legend.
All my nights are yesterdays.

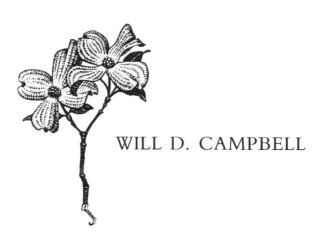

WILL D. CAMPBELL

Just Like Charles

Eulogy for a Child Who Lived to be Seven Years Old

We cannot say that he belonged to us. For nothing that has life belongs to anyone. It comes as a gift, as a matter of grace, and when it is gone, we cannot preserve it. And what was given to us so freely, we grudgingly return, but without apology, for the grudge is that difference which distinguishes the Divine from the mortals.

He only stayed a little while. But then he only came to stay a little while. For those who invited and hosted him during his stay among us knew that he couldn't stay for long. But they knew also what few of us ever learn—that sweetness of the visit is not determined by length or brevity of its duration.

His was a life of near reality—sand castles far enough removed from the surf to be still standing in the morning, cookies baked for God with a trace of doubt as to the ability of The Invisible to eat them, pet names like "Ole Poot" for his grown-up baldheaded friend, love and remembrance of music when others thought it bad and forgot it—a life of sanity and reality, unmarred by the dark groves of lunacy which engulf the rest of us.

He only stayed a little while. But it was long enough. Long enough to cry so as to know the joy of laughter, to suffer pain enough to revel in its absence, to contemplate the stars as nothing more and nothing less than stars, to hold in his grasp friend and kin who now mourn and mark his passing. And long enough to be remembered as one who dwelt among us.

Man and science labor long and hard for a day when Charles would have been just like us. The Almighty, in His infinite wisdom and mercy, has provided a day and time when we all will have been, and will be,

JUST
LIKE
CHARLES.   Amen.

The Death of Willie Gene Carreker

Woodland, 1974—During the decades of its heyday, the civil rights movement by-passed Talbot County, Ga., and in many ways it was a surprising oversight. One of the movement's major components, the Southern Christian Leadership Conference, was born a hundred miles to the west and was headquartered 90 miles to the north. In addition—and perhaps this was one of the problems—Talbot County had the third highest proportion of blacks of any county in the state.

Early this summer, while the ratio was still the same, the movement came. It came in the same form as it had come to Montgomery, Albany, Selma, St. Augustine, Birmingham and scores of other towns and counties. It came with the same tactics and strategy—marches, mass meetings, and economic boycotts. And it came too late to save the life of at least one black citizen, Willie Gene Carreker.

Its stay was brief compared to the others. But the victories it gained were in excess of most. And, in the relative scheme of things, the victories that may yet come could be almost revolutionary.

The Legacy of Matthew Talbot

Talbot County was born, if not of royalty, then certainly of aristocracy, and its history since its earliest days has been inextricably tied to the institutions of white supremacy. Created by the General Assembly shortly after the shaky and controversial Treaty of Indian Springs in 1825, it very soon proved to be ideal for growing cotton. And if cotton, then slaves. (Twenty-three years after its creation as a county, almost 9,000 slaves were listed out of a total population of slightly more than 16,000.)

The county was the namesake of Matthew Talbot, direct descendent of the Earl of Shrewsbury. Matthew's father, John Talbot (also the name of the first Earl), had bought 50,000 acres of land from the Lower Creek Indians. An Englishman brought over to survey it, George Walton, later became a signer of the Declaration of Independence. Eli Whitney, a teacher of Talbots' and other children on the property, invented the cotton gin in a little shop near the schoolhouse. Though his father's plantation was not within the boundaries of the newly created county, Matthew Talbot had been governor of the state for a short time and the county was given his name.

Lazarus Straus, who later founded Macy's Department Store, had been an early freedom fighter in his native Bavaria. When that revolutionary movement failed, he fled to America and through a series of circumstances settled with his family in Talbotton, the county seat. While he had actievily opposed European tyranny, he prospered in the new country and apparently was offended by neither the oppression of the Indians nor the tyranny of American slavery. The three sons of Lazarus Straus—Isidor, Nathan and Oscar—became more than famous sons of Talbot County, Ga. They went on to take their places in the fame and prominence of American history—in the fields of commerce, medicine, and diplomacy.

Within two decades, Talbot County became one of the most cultured and prosperous counties in the state. The aristocracy would see that their issue were educated. So private academies, institutes and colleges sprang up and served the wealthy of several states.

But with the Civil War and the end of slavery, the advent of the boll weevil and the demise of a cotton economy, the beginning of public schools and the bankruptcy and closing of the private academies and colleges, the ravishing of the pine timbers between the two world wars which had rapidly taken over the uncultivated cotton fields, Talbot County declined to today's skeleton of former wealth and splendor. It has approximately one-third as many people today as it had in 1850.

It is, of course, a familiar Southern story. What makes it a bit different is that until recently its ways were unchallenged by the civil rights movement.

The Lynching of William Carreker

Four individuals, two with the same name, one with no name at all, the other with one of the most distinguished names in the county, can be mentioned as landmarks in the long journey from the Matthew Talbot of 1827 to the coming of the movement in 1974.

In the spring of 1909 an elderly black man dressed in seersucker pants, black silk coat, red vest and red derby hat was the only passenger arriving on the train from Atlanta. Almost totally blind, he carried a well polished walking cane, and the gold watch chain across his chest made him something of an unusual sight for those at the depot in Talbotton, Georgia. Though he was known by no one in the town, black or white, he was taken in by a prominent black farmer named William Carreker.

It was not long until the white planters noticed a deteriorating attitude on the part of their colored people, and having just gone through the scare of the populist movement, the aristocracy put its intelligence in the black community to work. It was said that the old preacher was preaching to the local blacks about their continued state of slavery to the white man, telling them that if they would declare their independence they would be "free" as he was free and could wear a gold watch and diamond ring even as he.

The whites decided that some corrective measure was called for, and their decision was implemented quickly. A Committee of the People, what today would be called a mob, formed on Sunday afternoon on the grounds of the Methodist Church. On the following Saturday evening, about fifty men on horseback called at Carreker's farm and informed him that they feared insurrection and that they were there to flog the old preacher and make him leave the county. Only one spokesman, a wealthy landowner named Will Leonard, had approached the door. The others had remained in the shadows of early evening. Carreker asked that the old man not be hurt, explaining that he "didn't mean no harm. He just ain't got all his wits about him." When Leonard persisted and motioned for the group to advance, a shotgun blast from just inside the door dropped Leonard to the ground, his head separated from his body.

The Committee adjourned with considerable haste, not anticipating such a development at the home of so gentle a black citizen as William Carreker. But by Sunday afternoon it had regrouped with numerous additions from several counties. The body of Will Leonard had already been found at the Carreker front door, the hogs rooting and feeding on his brains.

Within a matter of hours the nameless "old preacher" had also been found—hiding in a sack in a nearby barn. He was hurriedly bound and weighted down and taken to a bridge spanning the Big Lazar Creek. Whether he was shot before, during or after his plunge into the water is not certain. But his body was found four days later a half-mile downstream, the gold watch chain glistening in the sun.

Two days later the befriender of the mysterious preacher turned himself in. But that night he was taken from the jail by a mob and next morning the body of William Carreker, who had meant only to entertain a stranger, was found swinging from the cross arm of a telephone pole on the courthouse square.

A brief account of the lynching was reported in the June 24 issue of the *Atlanta Constitution*, concluding with the statement that ". . . when the doors were opened it was the work of but a few minutes to get the negro. It was all done quietly and in perfect order."

William Carreker was buried by his family and neighbors. But the blind preacher who had come proclaiming justice and freedom left neither name nor shrine. The place and manner of his interment are not known.

A cradle native of Talbot County who also preached justice and freedom fared some better but received little acclaim from his neighbors. Clarence Jordan was born into one of the most prominent white families in the county. His father was a banker and merchant. His brothers are today important figures in local industry, agriculture, commerce and law. One brother, State Supreme Court Judge Robert H. Jordon, wrote a history of the county, *There Was a Land*, from which, along with other oral history, the above account is summarized. In it, Clarence Jordan rates nothing more than a listing.

Clarence went to the University of Georgia and studied agriculture. He decided early that there was something terribly wrong and unChristian about the system of segregation and discrimination in his native land. At the Southern Baptist Theological Seminary he learned to read the Bible in Hebrew and Greek, probably the first of his county to be able to do so since Lazarus Straus read it in his store and living room to visiting Methodist and Baptist preachers who could barely read English.

Jordon earned a Doctorate in New Testament, became an ardent pacifist in the midst of World War II and returned to a neighboring county to establish a communal and interracial community called Koinonia Farm. While at first he gained some acceptance as his contribution to improved agricultural methods in the area were realized, his community later became a center of controversy and violence. Barns, stores, and smokehouses were burned, residents were fired upon and exclusion from local churches soon developed into a total economic boycott during which those who lived at Koinonia could purchase absolutely nothing in the county and the town of Americus, not even the services of a physician.

Jordon preached total integration of every facet of society, opposed war in any form and through the example of communal ownership of property confronted the entire American economic system with his understanding of the Biblical Faith. He received few accolades from his peers in the white community at the time of his death in 1969. But he left many converts throughout the world, and even in life was counted a prophet, though without honor in his own town and among his own people.

The Killing of Willie Carreker

On the night of June 28 of this year several other names in the stuggle for equality emerged and a new chapter was begun. Another black man, also named Carreker, met a violent end. But times have changed. Or so they say. This time he was not lynched. He was killed by a police officer after being stopped for a traffic violation.

Only one man knows how it happened and it is doubtful if even he knows it exactly. There are now many versions and the following one borrows from several others. Police Chief Doug Watson and Officer James Mallory, the entire force in the little town of Woodland, were sitting in their patrol car slightly after midnight when they heard what sounded like a crash on the other end of town. When they arrived at the vicinity of the noise they found only tire marks and an electric pole at the intersection which obviously had been hit by a vehicle.

Assuming that the car had entered a housing project less than a block away they waited for it to return. As it did, they pursued it, concluding as they followed that the violator was drunk. After making one left turn they pulled the car to the side and recognized the driver as Willie Gene Carreker who lived about a block away on the same street.

They gave him the balloon test for alcohol content and placed him under arrest. When he protested, one of the officers radioed for the assistance of a state trooper. Apparently Carreker then agreed to be taken to the Talbotton jail and was placed in the back seat of the police car. At that point the trooper was notified that he was not needed. Officer Mallory was to follow the Chief in the Carreker car. But when Chief Watson went around to enter the driver's seat he found the door open and Carreker retreating into a corn field. Watson gave chase, and reported later that about twenty feet into the field Carreker shoved or wrestled him to the ground, that they had tussled and that his gun had gone off. He later admitted that he had drawn his gun when he ran into the field. He consistently denied that he fired the shot on purpose. But whatever the case, twenty-four-year-old Willie Gene Carreker was dead at the end of a gun, almost sixty-five years to the day since his great-uncle had died at the end of a rope seven miles away.

When William Carreker died, his family could do no more than grieve and give him a Christian burial. When his namesake and nephew joined him in death six and a half decades later, there was at least some recourse, some slight possibility of making his death count for something. His widow journeyed to Atlanta, where her husband had worked for General Motors, sought an audience with the Southern Christian Leadership Conference and was assured on the spot that the resources of SCLC would shortly be made available to the black community of Talbot County.

The Movement Arrives

Within twenty-four hours, Tyrone Brooks, National Communications Director of SCLC was on the scene to begin organizing the community. What he found was not as easily assessed as the situation in places where the movement had worked ten years ago. Despite the fact that the movement had never been active in Talbot County there had nonetheless been some changes. Issues were not as clear. Grievances, though still quite real, were more difficult to prove and state. Enemies were not quite so set apart for all to see. Claims of injustice and oppression could be countered with claims of recent gains and changes.

Brooks found a place where many black people are addressed by such names as Punkin', Sop, Snap, Dollar Bill or Waterboy. And the black principal of the county high school is still referred to as "'Fessor" by even the most enlightened whites. And yet 'Fessor was making more than $14,000 a year and was principal of *all* the children who went to public high school.

In short, it was a more subtle yoke and it is more difficult to organize and demonstrate around subtleties. But organize and demonstrate they did, for most of the ingredients were unmistakably there. A man was dead at the hands of a law enforcement officer in a county where 67 per cent of the citizens were black but where all police officers were white. Most, though not all, jobs held by blacks were menial. Most elected officials were white and most decisions affecting public policy were made by white people. Most blacks continued to be poorly educated, (though a sizeable number had been recruited to an unusually good Upward Bound program at Mercer University and a large number stayed on for college).

So Tyrone Brooks went to work to structure a movement. One by one issues were isolated and initial demands made, demands carefully designed to elicit umbrage from the white power base. (If folks won't resist you, you can't beat them.) First, Brooks and his followers announced that the police force of Woodland must be fired and the death of Willie Gene Carreker investigated and presented to the Grand Jury. To effect that, the body and burial of the victim became the focal point. Marches every day. A mass meeting and march every night. People too young to remember when Martin King, Jr. was alive, let alone the words to "We Shall Overcome," were carrying picket signs demanding FREEDOM! A local chapter of SCLC was formed and local leadership installed. An economic boycott against all white-owned and operated business was launched and proved to be one hundred per cent effective—so effective that a settlement was almost reached before the movement could get underway and state other grievances.

John Goolsby, owner of the largest market in Woodland talked freely and easily, one day recently, about the boycott. "Oh, yes, it's effective," he said. "Very effective. One hundred per cent. Not one black customer came in. I know—I make my living off black people. Always have, do now and always will unless I sell out and move on. But this is my home. I live here and my people lived here. I'm not going anywhere. But they're pretty much right. Of course, I have always had black people working for me. The first person I hired twenty-two years ago was black. And they have always been treated fair. A lot of the folks doing the picketing and leading the boycott hated to boycott me. In fact, some of them called and said they thought they could arrange it so my store would not be picketed. But I told them if everyone else was going to be picketed then I ought to be picketed too. After all, I'm white too.

"Now I could have sold a lot of stuff out the back door. But I've never asked anyone to come in my back door before and I'm not going to do it now. You know, my kids still go to the public schools. There's only nineteen whites in that school of eight hundred, and two of them are mine. But I don't send them there because I have black trade. I send them there because it's right and that's the way we have to educate our children. Of course, I've been criticized for that too. And I'm proud of my church in this thing. You know there was a meeting to form the bi-racial meeting (one of the early demands of the movement), and it was held at the Methodist Church. First one and then another was being nominated to serve on the committee. My little daughter got up and said, 'Maybe I'm out of order but my Daddy always taught us not to hate anybody, and I'd like to nominate my Daddy to serve on the Committee.'"

His voice broke and he drifted away, losing himself in the counters of his near empty supermarket. Gaining his composure he returned and continued to talk.

"And some folks, black and white, criticize me about Waterboy there." Waterboy, an elderly black man who couldn't talk, stood just outside the door, occasionally drifting in and out, giving the impression that he didn't understand what was happening. "Waterboy has worked for me for twenty-two years. I've taken care of him ever since I've been in business. You know what he did before that? White folks would give him a half dollar on Saturday evening to holler, just to make a blood curdling noise in his throat and folks would cheer all over town because they could hear him—like a fog horn you know. I can't pay him much but it's better than a human being hollering for a living. He had a stroke or something like that left him like that and he doesn't have much mind. And that's the only thing that I really disagree with the demonstrators on. When the picketing first started some of them would tap on the window and try to get him to come outside to join them. I called the leaders and told them Waterboy didn't understand all that and that they had to leave him alone."

John Goolsby stood for a long time, just looking at a sixty-year-old man whose only known name in the community is "Waterboy." He didn't say it but he is obviously content to let others judge and condemn this *noblesse oblige* of a bygone era. He didn't say it but he seemed to know that some of those who judge, expose and condemn such practices might well have had Waterboy in some drab and miserable institution long ago, where at least he would have been out of sight.

Goolsby talked some more about his black cashier calling every morning during the boycott to ask if he should come to work, and how he advised him each time that he thought he should support the boycott and stay home. And he also said he hoped the tragedy of Willie Carreker would not shoot an arrow through the good relationships that a lot of black and white people in Talbot County had managed to build.

The Emotional Peak

The movement continued to gain strength. Five hundred people on the main street of Woodland, Ga., is a lot of people. Night after night they were there, chanting, singing, handclapping and marching in front of where white folks sat on the ante-bellum porches and under mobile home awnings to escape the heat of Georgia July evenings with Tyrone Brooks calling on his bullhorn for them to join his people. None did.

The crescendo came a week later when Willie Gene Carreker was buried. The funeral procession took the form of a march from Talbotton to Woodland, the site of the dying and the burying. The Atlanta *Inquirer*, a black newspaper which had run a picture of the body of Willie Gene Carreker lying nude on a mortuary slab with the coarse stitches from the autopsy forming a grostesque "V" from the clavicle edges to the navel cavity, reported the number in the processional march at more than 1,000. The Columbus *Enquirer* called it at 200.

Either figure is a lot of people to walk seven miles on Georgia Highway 41 in July, especially for those taking turns carrying the casket. But either figure left a lot of black people *not* marching also. Many of those not marching lined the sidewalks of Talbotton as the procession filed by. They were called upon to join in, often by name. Some did, but most were content to stand and watch. One elderly black man was heard to say to his friend beside him. "Ain't you going out there and walk on the water?" The content and tone of his question seemed to suggest that it would take more than a walk to Woodland to alter his life now.

With the emotional peak reached and over, there was the more difficult task of settling on other specific issues, making demands and sustaining the boycott. It was the crucial period. Passion week had to produce an empty tomb or there would be no movement. Young Mr. Brooks was not unmindful of the danger as he set about the task of directing that movement in microcosm. The death of Willie Gene Carreker *had* to remain central. And it did. The police force of Woodland *must* be fired. This was to be the first demand. It would not be withdrawn and it was not negotiable.

Brooks had a lot going for him. But there were two important ingredients missing—national press coverage and a visible enemy. In earlier years when a black person was killed in the civil rights struggle, the nation could keep abreast of developments on the hourly news. Reporters, live microphones and camera crews filled the villages and small towns. It is easier to get the troops out if they are apt to be on national television that night. The death of Willie Gene Carreker got no such coverage. An executive producer of NBC News summed it up when asked why his network took no notice of the death and subsequent events: "A white officer shooting a black man is not news," he said. "It wasn't news twenty years ago. It *was* news ten years ago when the movement was big. But now it is *not* news again. It has lost its sexiness. In the first place we didn't even hear about it."

Others gave similar responses—not news. We didn't know about it. The public isn't interested. The civil rights movement is over. Whatever the reason, Tyrone simply couldn't get them there. He held press conferences, spent hours on the telephone informing them of what was happening. But they didn't come. So he had to go without them.

The other missing ingredient—a visible enemy—could be partially overcome, he figured, by simply creating or naming one. Brooks knew that people just won't march when you talk to them about the military-industrial complex messing over their lives. And you can't get them to sing freedom songs directed at the national power conglomerate. In the first place those things won't rhyme and the meter is always misplaced. But people will march, and they will sing, about a brutal, white Georgia sheriff. Therefore, the sheriff became the enemy.

> No more Sheriff Hendricks.
> No more Sheriff Hendricks.
> No more Sheriff Hendricks over me,
> Over me.
> Before I'll be a slave, I'll be buried in my grave,
> And go home to my Lord and be free.

> Freedom! O, freedom!
> O, freedom over me,
> Over me. . . . . . .

Try substituting "military-industrial complex" for Sheriff Hendricks. Try singing it to the tune of "O, Freedom!"

So Sheriff Charles Jefferson Hendricks became the target enemy. But it was bad casting. Jeff Hendricks just doesn't fit the part of the "typical Southern sheriff, noted for his viciousness towards blacks and his hard attitude towards the black community as a whole." He does carry a gun and he does wear a badge. But the gun hasn't been used during the ten years he has held office, and the badge looks more like the kind that used to come in Post cereal boxes than one belonging to the stereotype of a redneck lawman.

A conversation with the mother of Willie Carreker will reveal that she considered Hendricks generous and kind when she was held in his jail two years ago awaiting trial for the murder of her husband's paramour, and that when her son was killed it was Sheriff Hendricks who sent his brother to the woman's prison where she is incarcerated to bring her home, and that it was he who arranged with the state officials to give her an extended furlough during the time of mourning.

A brother, Dean Joseph Hendricks of Mercer, who had recruited dozens of black teenagers for higher education and who had once been state president of the Georgia Council on Human Relations, was seen often at the sheriff's side. A sister is the only white teacher left in the high school from the original faculty. And the most cursory investigation will show that it was not a county deputy who killed Carreker, but an officer of the township of Woodland over which the sheriff has no control. Thus, one of the major pieces of criticism in the rhetoric directed at Hendricks was that his clothes—faded, ill-fitting khakis—were not those befitting his office.

To picture Charles Jefferson Hendricks as the most gentle of men would be in error. But to picture him as a man who delights in gunning down black people is also in error. The facts were that on the night of the shooting he insisted that two black citizens accompany him to the hospital to examine the body for signs of violence prior to the fatal shot, and that he worked quietly and efficiently in many areas of concern where his oath of office would not compel him to go. In a step toward social justice and a peaceful solution to the immediate problem he did whatever he could.

But sheriff served as visible enemy for the movement, an ingredient necessary for a movement to move. And Brooks could make a case that he had stuck to *truth* if not to facts. Generically, at least, he was right about a lot of county sheriffs.

On July 10 a Black Manifesto addressed to every official from the County Ordinary to the Farm Bureau was issued. It contained 20 demands, beginning with the firing and prosecution of the Woodland Police Force. A County Human Rights Commission had to be established. Black deputy voter registrars must be appointed to register anyone of age who stated that he or she wanted to vote. Names of streets had to be posted in the black community, roads and sewers improved at once, recreation for all children provided, and the new police force of Woodland had to be both black and white. A moratorium on white hiring was demanded until all public agencies had staffs that were fifty percent black. The county was given twenty-four hours to respond.

The response came first in the form of cautious promises and confused hedging. No one individual or group could make such far-reaching concessions. But that weakness of structure in the white community didn't concern the movement. "That's *their* problem!" the black leaders said. And the demands stood.

So quiet negotiations began and off-the-record agreements were reached. The two policemen resigned, saving face for the town which had been adamant in its determination that they would not be fired. Sheriff Hendricks arrested the two men and held them in jail overnight until they could be taken before a three-man Justice of the Peace court for a hearing. The justices ruled that the officers were acting in line of duty but the way was left open for a later hearing before a higher judge who could bind them over to the Grand Jury if he chose to do so.

The Larger Fear

Meanwhile, another type of revolt was seething in the community. There had never been a major lawsuit over integration of schools in Talbot County. In the mid-sixties there was one black student in the formerly all-white high school. Nobody noticed.

But in 1970, in order to comply with HEW guidelines the black and white high schools had to be consolidated into one. The white flight to private schools began. A year later the County Superintendent of Education, a cousin of Sheriff Hendricks, resigned and became principal of the leading private school. This pretty much ended white attendance in the public high school. In the fall of '72 the number of whites was down to 18 out of 800. The former principal of the black high school, Mr. C. B. King, Jr., then became the principal of the former white school which whites were free to attend but didn't.

This year King's contract was not renewed and considerable rumble was heard in the black community. In fact, some felt that it was this fact, more than the killing of Willie Gene Carreker, which accounted for the militancy in the movement. But King had been replaced by another black man, and it was difficult for the SCLC to make much of an issue over it. Mr. King, or 'Fessor King as he is still called (by blacks because they want to, and by whites because some find it easier than calling him Mr.) is threatening to call a black boycott of the high school, but that prospect alarms very few whites.

144

What does alarm them is the possibility of blacks gaining control of the school board. Under Georgia law the school board sets the tax base and can place it at any level so long as it does not go over what is permitted by the state.

While blacks were attending the last mass meeting about the Carreker killing, whites, and some blacks, were meeting to protest the suggested tax levy for the coming year. That gathering was presided over by the present school superintendent, a white woman, and was described as a "nasty affair with neighbor screaming at neighbor, and the superintendent threatening to resign." White property owners were angry at one of their own. But if the superintendent resigns, the prospect of a black replacement who would almost certainly support an even higher levy is far from encouraging to the white landholders.

Though none talked about it, this was certainly one factor in the mind of the county and city officials who gathered at the Talbot County courthouse on Friday night, July 26 for a scene never before witnessed in that or many other counties in the South. White leaders, one by one, stepped forward and signed a covenant agreement to meet the terms, all the terms, of the Black Manifesto of July 10. It took longer than the twenty-four hours the movement allowed, but all demands were met.

One large landowner willing to talk, though insisting that it was the goodwill prevailing on both sides that led to the settlement, added a bit of his own thinking. "Up until now," he said, "it's been pretty much a matter between the colored people and the crackers. It really didn't concern us. But if they (the blacks) are the ones deciding what our taxes will be I might as well sell out now."

Epilogue

Late on a Friday night a small group sat in the weekend lodge belonging to Dean Hendricks, the sheriff's brother. There were black and white participants, critiquing the movement and trying to work out the "Fessor King" problem before it gets any bigger. Dean Hendricks was addressing the blacks, half, but only half, joking.

"Well, now, I just have to say one thing to the movement. You shouldn't have made fun of the Sheriff's clothes. That hurt the ole boy."

"O, hell. You know Joe, folks get kind of carried away."

145

It is hard to imagine that conversation taking place in Neshoba County, Miss. Or in Selma, St. Augustine or Albany. If it is not a new day, then it is at least a different day, where old strategies have been greatly overhauled. And it is hard to win when there really isn't much of a prize available to the winner. The struggle was really still over who gets the hamburger. It was not, and never has been, over who gets the filet. The landowner was right. It hardly concerned him at all. It was pretty much between the store and the trade, the pulp-wood broker—who happened to be the mayor of Woodland—and the pulpwood hauler, the sheriff and the blacks in the streets, none of whom are wielders of much power.

Or maybe that is the only power that will ever be up for negotiation. Whatever the case, the notion making the rounds in the early 60's that the movement had to do with a redistribution of America's wealth and not with buying a hamburger and a cup of coffee never got off the ground. Dr. King didn't get it off the ground nationally and Tyrone Brooks didn't get it to fly in Talbot County, Ga. The fight never reached the sirloin level. The fight was, and is now, over the hamburger and who gets which part of it. The blacks and second-echelon whites of Talbot County worked the things out that were theirs to work out.

The nameless blind preacher and Clarence Jordan would have been proud. But unfortunately, so would the Earl of Shrewsbury.

PAT DICKEY

Monarch of the Closing Green

Under the hawk sail there is an expanse
Of closing green
Which runs on to a pine selvaged ridge.
It is here I watch a memory beckon as sweetly
As northlight laying moss on stone.
Wind lifts the calling where the Georgia sun
Seduces the earth. It is
In this place I remember him most clearly.
Not caught up on day sound's distraction—
The monumental roar of determined folk
Running paved ribbons from here to there,
There to here,
He wandered oblivious to it all,
Dug at the old War.
Wearing a faded jacket with a peaked hood
The young hob man dissolved
In and out of slant light as it
Laid down bars of shadows on his back
Striped him until he all but disappeared.
I watched him because
There was nothing else to do but wait
Not understanding it much
This stacking more years in search of the collection
Than for any other concern of his time.
Still he crosses the dry river cut of recall,
Walks the run, the breastwork,
Thrashing distantly
Bent over the only weapon which can defeat
A century and more of hiding.
Tom listens to the piercing cry of the White
Strike its beam on grave bound iron.
Fleetingly glimpsed, woven into the trembling leaves
He pulls the headset down 'round his neck
Retrieves a shovel from his belt

And slams it into the damp-dark clay
With the frenetic power of a pirate who knows
There is only so much treasure left to find.
The topo maps have told him rightly.
Pine straw flies away from the War below.
Ching!
A bright blue bell of metal sparking metal sings.
Now he kneels to the task, large hands digging
The final distance with canine fury.
Then from the South-blood earth the thing
Is delivered back into the air which brought it
Here to Nickajack Creek from a Union gun.
Satisfied, he taps the clay from the phallus of the fuse
Pleased that the gunpowder is still within and battle ready.
As the dirt drops away, a Hotchkiss shell reveals itself
Yet another relic of one blazing Atlanta day
Decades' ghost.
He turns it, covets its weight and shape then
Eases it into a thready canvas bag
Back-hung and already heavy.
Carefully, with the slyness of a Potowatami,
The hunter heals the earth by chunking it in upon itself
Smooth scattering undergrowth over the scar.
The projectile king resets his ears
Grasps the White and hits his sweep again
Moving steadily among the trees.
He is as surely gone from me now as any sign of the War
Here under the hawk sail.
Relicker haunting the heart somewhere beyond the closing green.

RICKS CARSON

Red-Winged Blackbirds

You rose so in unison,
I thought some
fisherman had drawn
his net around you—
or that you
were the net: string,
knots, mesh.

The scarlet at
your shoulder, glimpsed
in a banking swerve
like blood in the wings—
mosaic hardening
in sky: witch's
sabbath cloak
without a seam:
flock of birds in
the fourth dimension.

To An Infant Found Suckling Its
Dead Mother's Breast

Rock blown as lightly as dandelion spoors
by the earthquake
against your mother's spine
probably disturbed your sleep, though in
death's briefness her muscles
drew up to cheat the shock that
would crush your paper skull.
You thought that she thought
you were hungry. So with a mouth
as formed for suckling as a sky
for holding light, you found
her breast.

Did the milk run dry before
it grew chill? At her marble skin
you continued for two days
to ply your lips, your tiny fingers
glowing like candles against the
still shrine of her throat.

Then the rescue team reached you.
With a shovel handle they pried
her stiff arms open and lifted you
wailing up toward light.

DONNIE D. PORTERFIELD

The Gleaning of Pearlie Mae

The woman stood at the kitchen sink staring through the dusty window into the backyard. Sighing she sloshed a nondescript piece of clothing in rinse water, wrung it out and dropped it into a dishpan at her feet.

"If it don't rain soon, Ma, I think I'm gonna' be crazy out here at the end of this old dusty road."

Wiping her hands on the front of her overalls Pearlie Mae rolled down the sleeves of the man's work shirt she wore and moved across the room.

A slight breeze came from a window where sagging, torn lace curtains waved weakly at the hot, Georgia day. In front of the window was a rocking chair which made small swishing sounds as it constantly moved back and forth.

"Ma, did you hear me?"

Pearlie Mae leaned over and faced the small figure within the confines of the chair. Dressed in a high neck, dark dress the old lady twisted her hands, mottled and thin as parchment, in small bird-like movements in her lap. The face, partially hidden by a shawl despite the warm day, hung with folds of loose sagging skin and smacked of the handiwork of a crazed sculptor who refused to stop applying his mortar.

The swishing of the chair continued as Pearlie Mae reached out and touched her mother's shoulder.

"Lord, Ma, I jest get plum sick of this old place. Don't you jest wush we could grow us some wings and jest fly on out of here?— Ma, are you listening to me a-tall?"

Shaking her head, the large woman straightened up, lumbered heavily across the room, retrieved the dishpan and started for the kitchen door.

"Git," she mumbled as she kicked at two chickens scratching in the dirt at the bottom of the steps. Moving across the yard her feet made little clouds of dust as she plodded toward a sagging clothesline. The hot, arid breeze blew the thin gray blonde wisps of hair across her full features. Heavily lidded eyes looked out from a round face dominated by a wide nose and pouting mouth.

Balancing the dishpan on her hip Pearlie Mae paused as she glanced back at her home. Standing back from a straggly lawn, fighting against an army of tall weeds was the big, unpainted frame house. The ragged screen surrounding the wide porch caught the reflection of the noonday sun and winked silver flashes through the limbs of giant oak trees. A derelict car, with three of its tires removed, leaned precariously against one corner of the sagging porch.

To the left of the house a crumbling shed housed an assortment of rusty cans, old cardboard boxes and various pieces of broken and discarded furniture. Protruding from among the contents was the rear of an ancient Ford coupé showing patches of its once blue color.

"Lord, this place is uglier than sin," Pearlie Mae said aloud.

A bumping, clanging noise caused the woman to turn toward the narrow road leading to the house through a maze of scrub oaks and kudzu vines. An old pickup truck with peeling green paint and a broken hanging tailgate made its way over the deep ruts and drew to a shuddering stop in front of the steps.

"Hot, ain't it, Pearlie Mae?" asked the man as he pushed open the creaking door and crawled down from the driver's seat. Equally as large as the woman he faced, the family resemblance was immediately apparent as he took off his baseball cap and the same gray blonde hair fell across his wide face. Wiping the sweat from his forehead with his sleeve he replaced the cap.

"How's Ma?" he asked.

Leaving the clothes Pearlie Mae caught up with him.

"She jest sets there a-rocking, Lonnie. She ain't said ten words in ten days."

Lonnie crossed the rickety porch and pushed open the kitchen door. The air became shimmery with heat as they walked further into the room. Going directly to the chair by the window the big man leaned over and spoke loudly.

"Ma, hey Ma! It's me—it's Lonnie."

"That ain't gonna' do no good, Lonnie. She don't say nothing. She jest sets there a-rocking."

Pearlie Mae pulled out a chair from the kitchen table and motioned to her brother.

"Set down. I'll get you some lemonade."

Going to the refrigerator Pearlie Mae got a pitcher, reached for a glass from the sink drainboard and set them down in front of Lonnie. She settled into a chair across the table and pulled a frayed newspaper clipping from her shirt pocket.

"Lonnie, I ain't exactly called you out here just to see about Ma. Doc Sam sez Ma's heart is strong. He sez she can go on a-rocking like this for years."

Shoving the clipping toward him Pearlie Mae took a deep breath.

"Look right here, Lonnie. When Mrs. Rutledge came by to pick up her eggs last week she brought me some old newspapers. And it sez right there in that piece that there's a new beauty school a-opening up right here in Waycross."

The swishing of the rocking chair seemed suddenly louder as Lonnie drained his glass and set it quietly on the table.

"What's that got to do with anything, Pearlie Mae?"

"Well, you remember when I was in high school I worked on the weekends in Miss Susie's beauty parlor a-shampooing and I really liked it. She was always a-telling me I had a natural talent for that kind of thing. So I thought maybe if I could go to this beauty school . . ."

"Pearlie Mae, you ain't been to high school for over twenty years."

"It don't matter, Lonnie. You don't never lose the talent and I done got it all worked out. I been saving some back from my egg and milk money and if you could just let me borrow a little from you I could hire Miss Lilly's daughter to look after Ma during the day and . . ."

Lonnie pushed his chair back from the table and stood up.

"You jest better stop right there, Pearlie Mae. There ain't no way I could get up nothin' that even smells like money. That wife of mine has done gone out and bought a colored TV on time and we still got two young'uns at home, you know."

The rocking chair seemed to swish a bit faster.

Lonnie pushed his cap back on his head and put his hands on his hips.

"You know I'm only on part time now at the mill, Pearlie Mae. God knows you've had it rough out here with Ma but there ain't no point in talking about no beauty school."

Lonnie walked toward the door and stopped.

"Pearlie Mae, for God's sake, you're forty-one-years-old!"

Sitting quietly Pearlie Mae heard the screen door slam, the truck crank and bump down the road.

Sometime later Pearlie Mae rose from the table and left the room. A few minutes later she appeared in an old army jacket with a battered suitcase. Taking the newspaper clipping from the table she stuffed it into a worn plastic purse and quickly left through the back door.

Running across the yard to the shed Pearlie Mae jerked open the door to the car and pushed the suitcase across the seat. Crawling in she blindly thrust the key into the ignition and began frantically pumping the gas pedal. After several attempts the motor started and Pearlie Mae backed into the dusty yard, thrust the gear shift into first and began the bumpy ride over the ruts through the scrub oaks and kudzu. Coming to the main road she banked sharply to the left and rolled onto the dirt surface. Pushing heavily on the gas pedal, Pearlie Mae succeeded in making the old car sputter and skip and slide in the soft sand. Twisting in her seat she felt the right tire slide into the road's shoulder and then slowly slip into the ditch.

Alternately stomping the clutch and gas pedal and twisting the key in the ignition, Pearlie Mae heard the car give one last shudder. Leaning her head against the wheel she closed her eyes and sat without moving.

Somewhere a dog howled and a bird, deep in the woods, trilled a sad, poignant sound.

Pearlie Mae got carefully out of the car and climbed out of the ditch. She began to walk and for a moment she thought she was getting somewhere. She believed the noise she heard was the suitcase slapping against her leg but when she looked up and saw the house again she realized the sound was the rocker, insistent in its back and forth movement, like a warped gate that never shuts just right and makes a weary sound in the wind.

MARTHA EDDINS BURGESS

Freedom

A lone stallion was just found
    Walking along the beach,
Reserved for lovers at this hour
    Of impunity.
They say it took four men with heavy
    Ropes to lead him off
And now, the profile of grim times
    Against gray tapestry,
He stands corralled and questioning
    Man's right to own the sea.

Love

I should be old enough to know
That embers die and coals grow old
But I sit giddy as a girl
Who knows no better than today
To hold the burning match away.

DEBORAH W. BURKHALTER

Jesus Saves! Jesus Saves!

After her bath, Susan Fields went out on the back porch where it was cool and looked up at the moon acting like somebody was holding it up so everybody could see how round and smooth and perfect and full of grace it was. The courthouse bell two blocks away chimed once. Amanda Jane was laying beside her, purring like the engine of Mr. Harry Leverette's shiny black Chevrolet next door. Amanda Jane's eyes gleamed cat-yellow fire against the blackness and the half-burned coals in the grill in the yard below glowed a soft gentle red as the pillows died their natural deaths.

There was a citronella candle burning on the table next to Nana's old wicker rocking chair and the scent of it joined with the scent of the honeysuckle that grew on the wire fence, making an exotic combination. Fireflies blinked off and on in the darkness.

Susan heard the clanging of a garbage can lid and knew Joe was home. He'd been working in Mr. Leverette's basement all day long and after supper he had gone out to the highway to clean up his patch of road.

Joe had this stretch of highway that he was always picking trash off of. It went from the corner where the A.M.E. Church was on down to where there was a sign that said "Drive Alive—55" and then he would stop. He wouldn't go no further than that sign. Every morning before breakfast and every night after supper, Joe would be down on his piece of road with an old croker sack and he would bend down and pick up beer bottles and cocola cans and cigarette packs and stuff that folks threw out of their cars. He would take the nasty old garbage home and then he would burn it all up in the oil drum at the back of the back yard and then it would be gone where it couldn't bother nobody no more. Joe knew what to do with trash. You didn't just leave it laying on the highway, you had to take it home and burn it and so that's what Joe did.

Joe appeared from behind their garage where he slept upstairs and he came over and bent down at the faucet at the corner of the house and he washed his hands and wiped them off on the seat of his pants.

"Peaceful out here, ain't it, Miss Sue?" He picked up a stick and poked at the dying coals in the grill and they glowed redder. Joe took

165

the stick, which had caught fire a little and was glowing at the end and he waved it around and around in a pretty figure-eight pattern and set it back down into the grill so it could burn up safe.

"That's real pretty. It's nice out here. There isn't anything else to do. It's too hot to stay inside the house."

Joe didn't answer but he dug into the pocket of his overalls and he had a piece of candy wrapped in cellophane. He walked over and gave it to her.

It was peppermint and Susan put it in her mouth and it was cool and bright and clean like a toothpaste commercial. She pushed it over to one side of her mouth and felt it poking out like she had the mumps.

"Thanks." She handed Joe the candy wrapper and he threw it into the grill where it melted and smelled funny when it burned.

"Welcome."

The little brass owl wind chimes overhead tinkled in the breeze. Joe got out his pipe and started fooling with it. He smelled like sweat and tobacco. They could hear Nana singing off-key in the kitchen, "We have heard the joyful sound, Jesus Saves! Jesus Saves!"

Joe looked at Susan and shrugged his shoulders and she giggled. Nana's singing was just pure awful. The neighbors would cuss and slam their windows shut when they heard her because she always did it real loud and real flat.

Joe handed Susan his pipe and the pouch so she could put the tobacco in and mash it down with her thumb. It was Cherry Blend and it smelled real nice. Joe always swore that Susan knew how to fix a pipe better than anybody he ever knew and he always let her fix it when she was handy. Joe leaned against the sidepost of the porch.

"What you doing over at Ole Harry's? What's he got in that old basement of his?"

"You don't call him 'Ole Harry.' It ain't fitten. You be getting yourself in trouble."

"Well, *Mister* Leverette, then. What's it like down there? Is it like a real dungeon? Can I help you tomorrow, Joe? Okay? Okay?"

"Well, I reckon you better ax Miz Fields first. You ax your Nana. What you want to do in that old basement anyhow. What you want to go and get in all that mess for?"

166

"I want to see what's down there. No telling what's in there. Old Lady Leverette might of hid her jewels down there before she kicked the bucket."

Joe laughed and struck a match and held it to his pipe and sucked. The fire in the bowl of his pipe glowed red.

"It's just a pile of old magazines and they all smell funny and old clothes and broke furniture and stuff. He wants the whole mess hauled up and burnt."

"Well, can I? Can I help? There's never nothing to do around here. Can I help?"

"Best ax your Nana," and he just looked up at the moon and they listened to Nana's singing and the purring of the cat and the tinkle of the wind chimes and watched the fireflies blinking off and on, off and on.

*   *   *   *   *   *

The yellow porch light snapped on and the screen door moaned its way open. Amanda Jane jumped up and ran off across the yard. Nana sat down heavily and her wicker rocker chair groaned. Nana sighed.

"It sure does feel better out here. I got to where I just cain't stand the heat. We have just got to get a air conditioner to put in the kitchen window. The fan don't do nothing except stir up the hot air."

"They on sale over in Macon," Joe said. "Two hundred and fifty something dollars for a right nice one that just works on a regular plug. You don't have to get an electrician to put in a high volt plug so that's a savings."

"I'm getting the check in three more days and I got about a hundred or so in the coffee can. How long they on sale, Joe?"

"I don't know. I'm getting fifty tomorrow iffen I can finish up on Leverette's basement and you can have that and we can just call it rent money."

"Can I help, Nana? Can I help Joe tomorrow?"

"You'll just be in the way. And I cain't take your money, Joe—"

They heard a yell and some cussing next door. There was a crash of broken pottery.

"I'm gone drown you, you durned animal! OhmyGod! Look what you done! Galldurnit."

167

"Oh, Lord," Nana said. "Oh, sweet Jesus."

"You better get that cat and get her inside," Joe whispered.

The bushes rustled and Ole Harry's pale face peered through. He come fighting through the branches. There was a broken piece of flowerpot in one of his hands and the stem of a great big plant in the other. Ole Harry stalked across the yard. He was dressed in a black suit and a vest and he had on a watch chain that glittered golden in the yellow porch light.

"That durned cat of your has done it again and now she's done broken my India rubber plant!"

Nana stood up to try to calm the old man down. The plant was just hanging there, bleeding white stuff.

"Don't you come near me, woman. I'm just warning you, if you don't do something with that cat I'm gone tie a cement block around its neck and throw it in the Ocmulgee River!"

Susan was thinking bad things. "I hope you die and burn in hellfire forever and ever and ever and it better really burn hot and it better really hurt you mean old coot you old butt you old mean old you old and I hate your guts." But she didn't say nothing out loud because Nana would pull a switch for bad ugly sassy talking.

"No, Mr. Leverette, you better not do nothing to that child's pet. She loves that kitty and you ain't gone throw it in the river and you ought to be ashamed talking like that in front of this sweet child, you old . . ." Nana breathed in hard. "I'll pay for that plant. I know they cost a lot of money and I'll pay for it. Don't you worry about that and I'm sorry it happened but you cain't talk like that around this here innocent child."

"Well. Just send your nigger over tomorrow first thing and see that all that mess gets cleaned up and we'll forget about the plant but I don't want to see that cat in my yard no more."

Joe stood up tall and his nose flared out like he was mad. Joe didn't like for folks to call him a nigger even if it was true. Nana said Joe was a colored man and Susan said he was a black man because her teacher had said it was backward and country to call them niggers and you should call them black even though they are really brown and it didn't make any sense to Susan but you better say black or else people would think you were countrified and redneck and so you better do it the way the teacher said. And anyway, Joe wasn't even

Nana's nigger, he was his own nigger, he was his own black man and so Joe was mad about it and so Susan was too. Damn Ole Harry Leverette straight to hell where he could just burn and burn forever and ever.

Amanda Jane jumped up on the porch and padded over to the door and Susan let her in. Ole Harry muttered something under his breath and turned around and went back to his own yard where he belonged. Susan ran over to Joe and he hugged her.

Nana and Joe sat back down and Susan went on inside. The breeze had gone down anyway and it had gotten hot again and she might as well go on to bed. She got in bed and fell asleep thinking about how in the world they made tires out of old plant juice. Nothing made any sense.

* * * * * *

The next morning, Susan ate a bowl of Crispy Crunchies with some peaches that Nana had put up in quart mason jars in June. Susan liked them because she had helped. They had all gone down to Fort Valley when the peaches come in and picked four bushel baskets full and they had peeled peaches for days and now there was a row of lovely yellow peach jars on the shelf. The next shelf down was tomatoes and it was always tomato time in the summer and the next one was string beans and they had about played out, Nana said, and now it was butterbean time and it was hot but Susan didn't like to shell them and that's why she wanted to help Joe. There wasn't anything to do and Nana would say well why don't you help me shell these here butterbeans and besides if she helped Joe they could get an air conditioner for Nana's kitchen. The peaches were sweet and good.

Joe come up on the porch and knocked on the screen door. "Hey, Miss Susan, you ready to come and help me?" he asked through the wire mesh that divided them but he wouldn't come in because that wasn't fitten and Joe never messed with things that he wasn't supposed to mess with and black men are not allowed in white ladies' kitchens because it isn't fitten.

"I got to tell Nana." Susan ran into the living room where Nana was polishing the furniture with stuff in a spray can that smelled like lemons and she was humming "Jesus Saves" or at least it sounded something like that, it was hard to tell with Nana because it didn't come out just right when she sung it, and it was a lot worse when she tried to hum it.

Susan told Nana and Nana said all right but she had better be back at dinnertime and remember she had to clean up that mess in her room sometime or other and maybe they were going to town later on.

Susan said okay and went out of the room but she stuck her tongue out at the picture on her way out. It was a picture on the wall of a pretty mama holding a baby that was Susan and there was a man standing behind them that was her daddy and that was who she was sticking her tongue out at. God damn him straight to hell. Any daddy that would just run off and leave a sweet little baby like that and a dead mama and not even put flowers on her grave and take the little baby to see her dead mama deserved burning in hell forever. That was trashy behaving to leave that little baby and so that's why Susan was sticking her tongue out at him. What kind of daddy was that? Trash.

* * * * * *

The screen door slammed behind her. Joe was cutting some pink roses from the bushes out by the corner of the house. Susan guessed they were going to visit Miz Joe again. She was behind the A.M.E. Church and there was a place beside her and for Joe with his name on the stone already but there wasn't any dates on it because he wasn't dead yet.

Joe picked up his croker sack and they went off up the street together. It was nice outside. The sun was shining but it wasn't hot yet. Mr. Chatfield was cutting his grass and it smelled green and fresh and Susan carried the roses that smelled like the perfume that the Avon lady had sold to Nana that she wore on Sundays or to town. It was called "Roses! Roses!" Susan thought about white pearls and white cotton gloves and Nana smelling just like roses as she nestled her nose in the flowers on the way to visit Miz Joe and to pick up the trash on the highway so Miz Joe wouldn't have to look at all that trash when she come out at night.

They put the flowers on Miz Joe's grave and then went out to the road and picked up a couple of cigarette packs and an empty bottle of King Cotton wine but that's all the trash there was on Joe's piece of highway. He didn't mess with any of the stuff past the highway sign.

A garbage truck come up that would swallow the trash up when the garbage man put stuff on the back. It had a motor in it that made a lot of noise when it ate the garbage up. It stopped and the man got off and got the garbage cans from people's back yards. Susan threw in the wine bottle and the trash and watched the motor thing turn inside itself and crunch up the trash like it was eating its breakfast or something. She held her nose because it stunk something awful.

*　*　*　*　*　*

All morning it was up and down and they hauled stuff up from Mr. Leverette's basement while he stayed inside and watched them every now and then from inside the house, with his face in the window like a man in a picture, all dressed up in a suit and looking like he was framed by the borders of the window and the curtains. Once Amanda Jane had come over but Susan took her home and put her in the house so she would be safe and she wouldn't end up at the bottom of the Ocmulgee River where it was red and muddy. Susan stuck her tongue out at Ole Harry Leverette's window when it was empty of his nasty old face.

The basement smelled funny, like something was dead down there. It was damp like a dungeon in a castle and Susan looked for rats but she didn't see any. There were trunks of old clothes and hatboxes. Susan tried on a wide-brimmed hat with flowers on it but it smelled funny and she felt creepy because she was afraid Old Lady Leverette would come back from the grave and get her for messing with her stuff. It was spooky down there and there wasn't any jewels either.

Susan picked up a stack of old National Geographics and took them up the steps to the daylight where it smelled better. She sat in the back of the yard near the honeysuckle where it was cool and looked at the pictures. There was pictures of nekkid little boys—little black boys from Africa. You could see *everything* and Susan studied them for a long time while Joe was carrying stuff up and down and putting it in a pile to be burned. Their mamas didn't have any shirts on and their boobies hung down to their waists and they had wires around their necks to make them long like giraffes. Once Susan felt somebody watching her and Ole Harry's face was at the window again. Burn in hell you old coot, she thought and she shut the National Geographic real quick so he wouldn't know she was looking at pictures of nekkid boys. Susan could hear Nana singing "Jesus Saves" again.

Finally Joe was through and he and Mr. Leverette set the whole pile on fire with kitchen matches. Joe had a shovel in one hand and his croker sack which he had wet down with a hose and slung across his shoulder in case the fire got out of hand. Nana hollered out the screen door for Susan to come get cleaned up because they were going to town to buy some material for school dresses. Susan hollered back "Okay, in a minute" but she didn't come because she wanted to stay and see the fire and watch it eat up the trash and burn.

It wasn't going good. Joe said it was because the stuff was damp from the basement. Ole Harry Leverette went out front to his car and got a can of gas, a red can of gas, and Joe told Susan she better stand clear because it was dangerous and Mr. Leverette poured the gas all over the stuff real slow and careful and it got going pretty good. There were some National Geographics and Life magazines scattered all over the back yard. Susan picked up one and threw it on the fire and it curled up around the edges when it died in the fire. The broken rubber plant was laying by the porch and she got that too so she could watch the white plant blood turn all black like it did when they made tires out of it and she threw it on the fire but nothing much happened and Joe said it was too green to burn good.

Susan picked up a stick and she put it in the fire until the end of it was glowing red and she poked around a little at the fire and sparks flew up like little fireflies only it was daytime and then she took the glowing stick and she swirled it around in a figure-eight pattern only the effect wasn't so fine in the daylight with the sun up there watching. Amanda Jane padded from around the corner of the house to watch and you could tell she liked it because you could see it in her cat eyes all narrow and searching like she would like to pounce on it but she was scared to.

Nana was on the porch at their house next door. She had on her black church dress and she was wearing her pearls. That was the way she went to town, like it was a funeral. Susan liked those pearls and she liked the smell of the "Roses! Roses!" that she put on but she didn't like the black dress because it was like a funeral and she just guessed Nana wore it to church because Jesus was still up there on that cross and it made Nana sad and so she had to wear black because it's the only thing that's fitten when somebody is dead or almost dead.

Nana was hollering and she meant it this time. "Susan, you better get yourself home and get some decent clothes on and you better do it right now!"

"Yessum! I'm coming!"

Amanda Jane was coming over to Susan and Mr. Leverette seen it. Oh boy. Amanda Jane got behind Susan and Mr. Leverette sprang. Amanda Jane leaped away real quick and knocked over the gas can and the gasoline gurgled out and it ran everywhere and it was all over the grass. Amanda Jane ran up on the porch and she knocked over a flowerpot with a red flower blooming in it and Mr. Leverette cussed "galldurnit" and he waved his arms and Amanda Jane got scared and she run up behind Susan again. Mr. Leverette was cussing real fine now and he even said the f-word and he said it again and he hollered that he was going to get that you-know-what cat if it was the last thing he ever done and he spun around after Amanda Jane who just stood there with her back up and her hair standing up straight and hissing like a cat does when it wants to cuss but it can't say any bad words and so it just hisses and sticks its back up like it is shooting a bird at you, you know how they are. And Mr. Leverette slipped on a National Geographic because it was slippery and he wasn't looking where he was going because he was mad as fire about that flower that Amanda Jane had broken and he fell down in all that gasoline mud where Amanda Jane had spilt it and Lord he was soaked in gasoline because he was kind of old and he couldn't get up real quick. And he was really cussing that cat and he sprang at her as soon as he was up and he got Amanda Jane by the tail and she screamed baby cat-screams and Susan screamed for him to leave that cat alone but he didn't and so she took the stick that was in her hand that she had been playing with that was on fire and she threw it at him.

It landed right about his middle and Mr. Leverette just flared up like he was a torch. It just ate him up, rising from his middle on up to his head, spreading fast but it seemed real slow like on TV when they slow the film down and you know that it is happening fast but it looks slow, and at the same time it was spreading from his middle down to his shoes but around his belt it didn't burn much, like he was divided. He screamed like a demon just let out of hell, just screams without any words that nobody could remember afterwards, it was just high-pitched and he stretched his arms out wide and he ran around like something wild around and around in circles with his body like a flaming yellow cross and Joe was screaming too, for him to roll in the grass, hit the dirt, where is that fucking sack and don't run and finally Joe wrastled Mr. Leverette down to the ground and they rolled over and over in the grass until Mr. Leverette was out. Nana had come running over and she just kept screaming oh, Sweet Jesus, Jesus, Jesus, save us sweet Jesus and Susan why did you do it you were always such a sweet child what made you do that oh sweet Jesus Susan how did you why and Joe get him get him Joe Joe that sweet child.

And Susan just stood there with her throat all closed up and she didn't cry and she didn't holler and she just stood there and she run up to Nana after Joe had Mr. Leverette on the grass and he was put out and he was just laying there still and quiet in the grass. And Susan couldn't hardly breathe and she didn't *mean* to do that but she was glad she had done it anyway and she was scared because she was glad and so she just put her head in Nana's breast while Nana was screaming all about her sweet Jesus and Susan was scared because she just knew that Jesus wasn't ever going to save *her* and she just hid her head in the black dress and smelled the scent of "Roses! Roses!" and the smell of the burning trash and the odor of gasoline and the sweet and nauseating stench of burning human flesh and she just stood there with the glacial fear that she had damned the man to hell and she had burned him and that it had hurt him and burned and burned and she had damned her own self too and she finally turned away from Nana and she shivered in the gaze of the sun overhead that saw the whole thing.

JOANN PETERSON FLOYD

Cane Grinding Time in Georgia

A gentle time, the caning night,
The bright stars etch the sky with light
And fire, from underneath the pot,
Flames bright, keeping the syrup hot.

Black folk press near quietly to reach
More skimmings, harvest time's release,
While children brag who'll eat the most
Of new syrup on the morning's toast;

Drink green juice from tin cups, a taste
Drawn from the press to one mule's pace.
The blacks and whites on country road
Enjoy the night, in autumn's cold.

No mad dog howls. The world seems right
This gentle time, the caning night.

A Bride Contemplates Love's Separations

Face pressed to glass, I watch you go,
Heart in my throat, because I know
Another Mistress calls you now;
Fame, dressed as Duty, woos—love's foe!

Fear whispers low, her voice unkind;
She speaks about a later time,
About the Rival yet to come
When Death will want . . . will claim . . . take . . . mine.

Insomnia

The clock
  clanging three
    is
the bugle call
    to
The Small Self kept hidden.
A Mouse
  who darts out,
    eats
the cheese until
  Dawn
appears, stifling freedom;
So Self
  emerges
    to
search for answers
  that
Daylight will banish.

JOANN PETERSON FLOYD

The Flight Over

Joanna, I, sit on a row, packed—
like tin soldiers—rigid, cold.
The airplane lifts into the skies.
The Latins—all but us—flash smiles,
Sing native songs across the miles.
We watch the priest pray with his kin,
The girls, demure, with olive skin,
men, handsome, dark, quick to embrace.
We feel alone, cramped in their space.
We wish we were some other place.
Until amid their happy noise one gives
Balloons to us, their toys.
They draw us now into their game.
They make us feel at ease again.
Sicilian party on the plane.

(To Mary who gave us balloons.)

On Viewing Mount Etna

The Mount, puffing smoke,
    is a peaceful sight
to the eyes of
    observers;
Like men who
    with pipes, sit awhile
with calm airs
    disguising danger;
So its appearance
    gives lie to the fury
that one day will rupture.

179

GEORGIA ON MY MIND

double haiku

seeing this child sleep
stirs memories of fragrance
of gathered flowers.

veins etch her eyelids,
delicate lavender lines
on Spring's white lilies!

JOANN PETERSON FLOYD

The Short Run

Zelda Jean's Chapter
Toomsboro, Georgia

The store is still here. The Short Run, it says, the words spelled out in neat, green letters over the door. *THE SHORT RUN.*

"If the run hadn't been short, I'd be dead, too, Luke, like you; dead like you . . . I am dead; but not like you. I wonder when you'll be back to dust and ashes—like the house across the street is now. They destroyed it, too, Luke. It's gone, as gone as you are. They destroyed it—poured kerosene, struck a match and burned it to the ground. They destroyed it, like they destroyed you. The house is gone. You're gone.

My God, what am I doing here?

Why was the run over here so short?

Why did I run anyway?"

Mrs. Dixon's Chapter
Toomsboro, Georgia

"There she is, Dix. Her shoddy ole station wagon's parked across the street. She's staring over here at the store like a whipped bird dog, more wild-eyed than your bitch Molly was when you found her quivering in the ditch that rainy afternoon.

What's gonna happen to her, Dix? God have mercy on the child. She's still looking this way. Maybe she's looking to us again, Dix. There ain't no one else for her to look to."

"I didn't think they'd go this far," Dix mutters. "He might as well a drove the axe in Zelda Jean's head. He's finished her off too, as sure as if he'd struck her with that axe. The old fool—dyin is too good for him. The way he lily-livered out of it, claimin Beulah Mae done it all.

If a man cain't stand up to a woman over nothin, even murder, he ain't fit to be called a man. If he had any backbone, he'd have locked Beulah Mae up years ago in Milledgeville where he's got her now.

181

The way he sneaked back over there in the dead of night a-pourin kerosene all over that house and a-strikin the match—I know he done it—and you know it, too. Jest as shore as the Georgia sun shines down on that burnt-out spot across the road, ole Ben Roundtree burnt the house down. He never knew nothin but coverin up—and I reckon that's what he was a-doin then—coverin up the blood or somethin. Sly ole fool.

Why does God ever give a child to fools like Ben and Beulah Mae? All they ever done was a-leadin up to what you see across the street now. Desolation and ruin. A house burnt to the ground and a daughter starin at it with nothin left but an ole rattletrap of a car. They was a-bullyin and a-whippin Zelda Jean from the time she was born. At least, that fool Beulah Mae was, a-bullyin her and a-hollerin about hell fire and damnation to the child if'n she wanted to wear lipstick or take off those ugly blue stockins or fix up like the other girls. And a-makin her study all day long Saddays without ever goin to a pitcher show or playin with nobody—or nothin. Ole Ben wasn't much better, standin round pullin on his suspenders and flickin cigar ashes off'n his nasty shirt front, a-figurin out how to cheat somebody. The only way you'd know he was a man was he wore britches. And then you weren't too sure. Lettin her boss Zelda Jean around, pretendin he didn't hear—why he must have jelly in his veins where the blood's supposed to be. The old crook. Never has, never been, nothin else. Remember how he'd use a stovepipe to put them sorry nuts in the middle of them see-through crocus sacks so as to make folks think they was buyin good pecans? How could a nice girl like Zelda Jean be born to a man like that—not to mention her crazy mamma?"

"Hush talkin, Dix.

Go out to the car and get her. Make her come in and have some cornbread and buttermilk. She's liked my cookin ever since she first crossed the road out there with her doctor kit and her Shirley Temple doll.

Go, get her, Dix."

JOANN PETERSON FLOYD

Luke's Parents' Chapter
(The Reverend and Mrs. Andover)
Philadelphia, Pennsylvania

"Grace, put your snow boots on before you get out of the car. The
ground is still icy around the grave. Here, let me help you. I know
you want to read it for yourself. Well, no, I'll read it to you.

"The Lord giveth and the Lord taketh away,
Blessed be the name of the Lord
Jonathan Luke Andover III, Physician
Born Calcutta, India, May 1941
Murdered, Toomsboro Georgia, March 1968
Son of Missionaries to India
Jonathan Luke Andover II
and
Grace Arrington Andover
Philadelphia, Pennsylvania
Husband of Zelda Jean Rou. . . ."

His voice breaks. "Grace, I'm not going back to India. I can't speak
of God's love in India—not the way I hate those God-forsaken folks
that did this to Luke. I hate them so I can't even say their names. The
Good Book says, 'How can you say you love God when you hate
your brother?'

And I hate those sorry rednecks that killed . . . our . . . How did
a child of theirs ever get as far as a Residency in The Women's
Hospital of Philadelphia? . . . How could all of this happen? Why?
Why?" His voice falters and his unsteady right hand fumbles for a
handkerchief.

His wife moves closer to him. The strand of gray in her dark hair
reminds him of her sacrifices. Still elegant and refined, with her old
gray coat tied around her thin figure, she holds on to him as they
look at the marker over their only child's grave.

"If he'd never met her, Grace, if . . ."

"But Jonathan, the Lord must have had it in his plan. That's what
you tell our people in India. You tell them that nothing can happen
without going by His drawing board, that God has a plan for . . ."

183

Her voice breaks and she buries her face in her husband's overcoat collar.

The Pennsylvania March wind blows its icy fingers up their coat sleeves, chilling them to their bones.

They look at the grave one more time. Clutching each other, they walk back to the rented car.

Zelda Jean's Second Chapter
Toomsboro, Georgia

Back at The Short Run Zelda Jean sits by the pot-bellied stove eating the corn bread. She doesn't appear to know she is eating.

Her dark tortured eyes stare blankly at her old friends. She retells the story to them as if she is trying to make some sense out of it . . . out of her life. She seems to be trying to hold onto her sanity.

She brushes the dark bangs out of her eyes. "Ma Dixon, I called Mama and Papa from Philadelphia. I told them about Luke. When they heard his folks were missionaries to India, they started yelling at me.

I tried to explain to them that Luke was not a Hindu, nor a heathen, nor an Indian. 'He was just born in India, Ma,' I'd say. 'He's a white man, like Pa is. His folks are from a distinguished Pennsylvania family. Only they went to India as missionaries in 1940 and Luke was born there.'

'He's a foreigner,' Ma would yell, 'a heathen of the worst sort, pretending to be a Christian. He's trying to take you across the ocean with them Hindus. Why, I've seen them queer religious folks paradin up and down the road here in Georgia in their white sheets, beggin for their bread. I didn't teach all them years at Upper Lotts Creek to send you up there to marry a dark-skinned heathen. You cain't marry him, Zelda Jean.'

'I'd marry Luke if he was black as the ace of spades, Mama. I love him and I'm going to marry him,' I told her. I stood up to her that once. That's when she went to pieces. So I called my Uncle Pete over in Waycross to ask his advice. You know he's mother's brother, the superintendent of the Morris County Schools. He said, 'Zelda Jean, your mother is crazy. Don't bring Luke to Georgia. If you marry him, stay away from Toomsboro, Georgia.'

But Ma Dixon, I didn't dream they'd kill him. So we were married in Philadelphia—without our families. But for our honeymoon we drove to Georgia. You saw us drive up two weeks ago.

When we walked into the house Ma said, 'So it's you, Zelda Jean, and your dark-skinned husband. Well, no flesh and blood of mine is gonna have a dark-skinned heathen husband.'

Luke looked at me. Before he could put the suitcase down or turn and leave or anything, she shot him. Right through the heart. Pa kicked Luke in the head with those big brogans of his. I was beating on Pa with my fists trying to stop him.

Ma Dixon, my mother turned the gun on me. Those black eyes of hers leveled straight at me and she said, 'You're next.'

What kind of crazy woman would shoot her own child?

Only she's not crazy, Ma Dixon, unless mean is crazy. And Pa . . . He said, 'Wait, Beulah Mae, don't shoot Zelda Jean.' He did say that. If he hadn't tried to stop her, I wouldn't be here either.

That's when I ran, ran, ran out of that hell of a house over here to you. Oh, thank you for hiding me under that meat counter.

Thank you for lying to them—for saying I had run through the woods to the creek.

Thank you, Uncle Dix, for calling the sheriff.

You saved my life. But why should I want to live? Why am I living? Luke is dead. They killed him. My own folks murdered him. And now Pa's in the hospital . . . dying . . . They think he has arsenic poisoning from those cookies Ma fed him when he visited her Sunday at Milledgeville.

Soon she'll be out. That blue stocking judge said Mama was temporarily deranged because her daughter took up with a heathen.

And I want to be dead, too.

I am dead.

"What will happen to me?"

The telephone rings, interrupting them. A distinctive Eastern voice asks, "Mrs. Dixon, do you know where we can find Zelda Jean Andover?"

"Zelda," she says, "this must be Luke's father."

Grasping the telephone, the young woman hears Reverend Andover say, 'Zelda Jean, my child, we know how our Luke loved you. Our hearts are all broken. But we must go on. We must finish our course. For years, we've prayed for a doctor to join us in India. That was our dream for Luke . . . Would you consider taking his place?"

After a moment of stunned silence, Zelda Jean sobs, "Father Andover, if I . . . if you . . . want . . . can."

Taking control of herself, she begins again, "Father Andover, Papa Andover . . . I will . . . I will . . . I must. Where shall I meet you?"

ROBBY LYNNE STROZIER

Life

Life is just a bowl of cherries
Only
Don't turn the bowl upside down,
Please . . .

Present

There is no present
    It is gone.
There is no past
    It is gone.
There is no future
    It is gone.
And so are you.

Round and Round

Round and round
Come ride the Merry-Go-Round
Of life.
Start things
Leave things
End nothing.
Begin . . . Begin . . .
No end in sight.
Too late.
Too late.
Now . . .
Death is waiting
With a doggy bag
To take me home
For her midnight snack.

No more

No more yesterdays
No more tomorrows
No more todays.
For there I lay
On the table
The main course
Looking
At death
Pick up
Her knife
And fork
And put me
On her plate
For dinner.

Bury

Life
Is not going
To sit and wait
At the terminal station
For you to hop
On the train
And ride with Spring
Into Winter.
But Death
Has reserved
You a place
In the caboose
And is
Waiting.
Patiently
On your ticket.

JOHN YOW

The Time Belle Run Off

My head's hurting so bad I'm scared to open my eyes so I'm laying there holding 'em shut tight and say to Belle, "Can't you make that goddam kid shut up?" Well, she don't answer. I stretch out a hand and don't feel nothing on her side of the bed and little Buster commences in again. He sleeps right in the same room in a crib the boss give to us and Jesus God that little feller can set up a racket. Me and Belle's got four now (biggest one turned six last month) and them others can holler too, but they all stay in the other room and you can shut 'em up in there when you need to. Well, I see I got to open my eyes even if it'll set my head to pounding so I let in the light of day and sure enough Belle ain't there. I step into the kitchen and see she ain't there neither and then try the kids' room. I tell you, what I see when I open the door makes me so sad and so proud I like to broke down crying right there. There is Jean Sue (she's the oldest) with nothing on but her little underpanties but she's got a ring of lipstick around her mouth and she's acting like she's feeding breakfast to the other two. She's playing at being their momma, don't you see.

"Hey little darling," I say to her, "where's momma?" That's all it took. Her little eyes start filling up and she's trying to be so brave and grown up but she can't hold back from crying no longer. She tells me Belle took out last night not long after I did and she was fit to be tied. She tells me Belle was screaming and hollering that she wasn't never coming back here no more, *never*. Well, I pick my little girl up and hug her and tell her don't worry, daddy's gonna go get momma and bring her back home but I'm wondering will I be able to keep my word. I tell you, I was getting right mad at Belle, too. Ain't no reason I shouldn't go drinking with Homer's daddy on a Friday night. I put Jean Sue down and go to the kitchen to get some milk for little Buster but there ain't none. There ain't much of a goddam thing, if you want to know the truth, so I don't wait around another second. God, she tears me up when she throws them fits, cussing at me and kicking at me and swearing she wisht she'd never married me. Sometimes I have to smack her one just to be able to talk some sense to her and then when I hurt her my heart just busts wide open. But better or worse that's my goddam woman and I'm

193

thinking as I'm walking up the hill to Homer's house if she's with another man there's gonna be hell to pay.

I knew Homer wouldn't help me, no use to even ask. Saturdays the boss always comes out to talk to him, but he wouldn't do me no favor nohow. I can tell he don't think much of me, thinks I'm lower'n him, thinks I'm a hillbilly. It was him give me this name, Dude. I know he's laughing at me when he calls me by it. Hell, he's alright, though. I've worked for lots worse. I just stop in to tell Homer Belle's run off and I'm gonna get the boys to help me go find her and he says its a shame to wake them boys up on their day off just like I knowed he would. But I say, "Shit, Homer, I can't just sit here and scratch my ass."

Now them boys is nice. John had him a old Plymouth, and I didn't have me no car at the time. I never could keep one. Ever one I ever had I'd just play with it till I broke it. Never had no driver's licents, neither. I always figured you had to be able to read to get any, but them boys told me if you go down there they can call out that test to you, so I'm planning on getting me a set one of these days. So anyway I head across the road to the house where the boys stay and I tap on the window where I know they're sleeping and after a while Jimmy lets up the shade and there I am. "Belle's done run off," I tell him. "I'm counting on you boys to help me find her."

I tell you, it ain't two minutes before them boys is dressed and outside the house and we're all climbing into John's old Plymouth, me and Jimmy in back and Steve riding up front with John. Of course they're wanting to know when she took out and where'd she go and all that shit, but I don't know no more'n they do. All I can tell 'em is, she might of headed back to her folks' place, up in the country north of Canton, and that's where I figure we ought to head.

We stop at a Seven-Eleven to get some gas and I try to give John some money but he won't take none. I knew he wouldn't. I reckon them boys don't need their money bad as I need mine, but still. By the time we get going again I've done opened the blade on my knife and put it back in my pocket and crumpled up a paper cup in my hand for padding. You got to hit somebody, it don't hurt near as bad if you got something in your hand like that. Don't hurt your hand, I mean. Jimmy seen what I was doing and looked at me funny, but I just smile at him like there ain't nothing to worry about.

I tell you what, these damn dirt farmers around here beat all I ever seen. Homer thinks I'm low class on account of I come from Carolina, but up there there's things for people to do besides scratch around in this old hard red clay. You ought to see it out there where Belle's folks live. Ain't nothing but red dirt and them sorry old pine trees and them folks out there ain't got a pot to piss in. The house Belle's folks live in looks like a pile of tar paper and scrap wood—hell, it ain't no better'n my house. But that don't stop 'em from looking on me like I was trash.

Well, we pull into Belle's folks' place and I get out of the car and lean in John's window and honk the horn. After a while the old man comes to the screen and seeing it's me he comes on out the door. Always was a ugly old son of a bitch. Wider than he is high, and got a big old red splotchety face. Ain't a single hair on his head and if his earlobes was any longer he could drape 'em over his shoulders. He's always got a big wad stretching out one cheek and the ends of his mouth turn down like they was headed somewheres. So anyway he asks me what I'm doing out his way and I ask him has he seen Belle. Well, I can tell by the way he takes his time spitting out that tobacco juice that he's fixing to enjoy himself.

"She's yore wife," he tells me. See what I mean?

Anyway, I tell him about how she's run off I don't know where and I was thinking maybe either him or Lum had come to fetch her.

Now why would him or Lum do that, he asks me. "You ain't been mistreating her, is you?"

Well, he's beginning to make me mad now, but I just tell him calm and level as I can that I don't know nothing about it, don't know where she went nor why. I tell him I just got to find her and bring her back home, is all. Kids was hollering when I left.

He eases up on me then. Tells me Belle ain't there and he ain't seen her ever since her and me was out there last. "Lum done gone off, too," he tells me. "Moved in toward town. I couldn't rightly tell you where." It's just him and the old lady out there now, he says, and I'm near to feeling sorry for him when I remember what a mean old bastard he is.

I say good day to him then and squeeze back in the back seat of the car, but before John gets moving the old man has done walked over to where the car's sitting. He puts them big old fat hands on the bottom of the open window and leans his red face down toward mine. He ain't ready yet, though. First he's got to let a big quid ease down out'n his mouth and got to follow it all the way to the ground with his eyes. Then he looks back up at me and says, "When you find her, belt her acrost the mouth one time for me. She ain't got no bidness running off and leaving them little uns." "Them's my grand-chirren," he says. I'm telling you, I didn't know whether to laugh out loud or bust his head open. He wouldn't give a fart in a feedsack for them kids.

Well, the boys is wanting to know if we're going to go looking for Lum, but hell, I wouldn't have no idea where to find him. And besides, there's one more place out here in the woods I want to stop in at. A rundown old body shop where some of them old boys works that used to go with Belle. Now this place is on up in the country a ways and it's already starting to get hot and I'm starting to feel bad about asking so much from them boys and that makes me even madder at Belle but shit, we've done come this far.

Even though I'd never been there but one time in my whole life I knowed we'd find it. I always could get back to any place I ever been. Something in my blood, I reckon. Well, after a while we come up on it, and it wasn't hard to recognize. Old tires, car seats, bump-ers, all kind of junk just throwed ever whichaway. And then I see them old boys eating their lunch over yonder under the shade tree. The one I'm looking for most ain't there, but I see old Buddy Wheel-er and he's just about as bad. Ain't none of these folks out here anything but mean, though. They'd steal a man's wife off just for pure pleasure.

Well, John pulls the car over toward the tree and I tell them boys not to worry, I doubt I'll be needing 'em, but why don't they just open up their doors anyway, and then I step out of the car. Sure enough, up jumps Buddy Wheeler from off the car hood they was sitting on and comes strutting right up to me. He ain't big as I am but you can see that don't bother him none.

"Well lookahere, boys," he sings out to them others. "If it ain't old William Lassiter, old Romeo hisself." See there? That's what they never could stand. It was me Belle chose and they hated me ever since. So anyway he says how I'm the one what stole *their* Belle away just when she was learning how to have her a good time. Now you know what that means. Well, I see this ain't gonna be no fun but I ain't about to give up now so I just come right out with it. I tell him Belle's done run off and I ask him to just tell me straight if he's seen her out this way.

Well, he commences to thinking about it. Looking back on it, I see he was just playacting—scratching his head, toeing the ground, squinching up his face like he was straining to remember—and maybe I knowed it then but I couldn't do nothing but hear what he had to say. "Naw, I ain't," he says, just when I think I'm gonna have to ask him again. "I ain't seen *Belle*." And here he makes a mean little laughing sound, just in case I don't know how much he's enjoying this. "But I tell you what I did see. I seen a pair of feet I could swear was Belle's sticking out the window of Olin Wilson's pick-up truck about dawn this morning, and the cab of that truck going up and down like a goddam . . ."

I didn't care to hear no more. By the time I've grabbed his shirt and yanked him up against me with my left hand, I've done pulled the knife out of my pocket with my other one and I'm pressing the flat of the blade against the tip of the son of a bitch's nose.

"You tell me right where I can find 'em or you're a dead man this minute," is what I tell him, and I mean I hiss it right in his face. Them other two old boys they jump up fast and my three boys hop out the car all at about the same time and everybody just holds what they got. And old Buddy, he changes his tune right quick.

"Shit!" he hollers. "Goddam, man, take it easy. I was only kidding." Of course I don't know if he's lying or not and I got a half a mind to kill him anyway so I'm still holding on tight, listening to my heart thumping. "Hey William, I swear it man." He's begging now, scared I'm gonna hurt him. "Olin Wilson's done settled down and got married himself," he tells me. "He don't even care about Belle no more."

Well, I'm cooling down a might and start to let go my grip but the second he sees that blade drop away from his face he jerks his knee up into my crotch just as purty as you please. I beller and double up and grab my balls with my left hand and just try not to black out, but when I turn my head to the side I see old Buddy ain't done yet. He's drawing back his leg like he's gonna kick my head off but I see it coming and his leg goes so high in the air it pulls the other one out from under him and he lands on his back so hard you could hear the breath knocked out. Then I fall on his chest knees first and starting at the corner of his left eye I open a gash all the way down his face to his jawbone. He would of let out a scream, I reckon, but just didn't have no air in his lungs. Kind of scares me now to think about what I done but at the time I didn't have no feeling I could name. It might just as well of been somebody else holding that knife.

I stand up then and groan some and grab hold of my nuts again and drag my ass back to the car. Them boys is coming too, ever looking backwards to see what them other two old boys is up to. Hell, they wasn't up to much. Time we was back in the car and rolling, one of 'em had gone to puking.

Well, we ain't found my Belle, but I ain't up to no more looking. I can't rightly tell you how I'm feeling. I ain't feeling sorry for Buddy Wheeler, I know that much. I'm still hunched over holding my balls and thinking maybe I should've cut his off but when I say that to the boys little Jimmy says, "Goddam, Dude, I sure am glad you didn't, else we might as well just drop you off at the jailhouse." But I ain't feeling good, neither. Trouble is, I'm heading back home without no wife.

I'm thinking about them children too so I tell John to stop off at the store so I can get 'em some milk. Then I tell them boys I believe I'll buy 'em a beer for helping me out like that. Well, they love that cause they ain't old enough to buy their own but of course they won't let me do no paying. We get us a couple of six-packs and I tell you, young boys like that, it wasn't long before they was laughing and cutting up, drinking to me and saying how I had really give that old boy what was coming to him. Hell, I didn't mind. They didn't know no better.

I reckon it's about two o'clock when we pull back into Homer's place, and Homer's down his front steps to meet us before we've ever come to a stop.

"You find her?"

I say hell no and ask has he seen her back over this way and he says, "Look yonder."

He's pointing back over his shoulder and sure enough there's Belle walking up to the screen door. Well, I kind of stare at her for a minute not knowing what to do and then I start getting out of the car and she starts pushing open the screen door. I can see now that her eyes are all red and the little corners of her mouth are trembly and I just throw out my arms wide open. I reckon I done right because here she comes, jumping down them steps and into my arms and hugging my neck till she like to broke it. I'm kissing on her like there ain't no tomorrow and I hear old Homer behind me saying, "Shit, him putting you boys to all that trouble just so he could have a taste of that sugar," and I have to laugh at that one myself. But then I hear him say in a voice like he's telling the saddest story in the world, "One thang's for certain, boys, number five'll be on the way directly."

I'll tell you the truth, though. I wouldn't of minded if it was.

CYNTHIA J. RICHARDS

Winter's Night

You pulled me out into the night
With cheeks bitten red by sharp, blue cold.
You pulled me from my warm, safe home
And through the solid wall of cold so hard
I felt the blow against my chest.
I gasped to fill my lungs.

Kicking up snow's fresh laid, downy bed,
You pulled me under streetlight's cold, white glow.
"Look!" you cried and flung your arms out toward the night.
Then slowly turning 'round, my breath was stolen clean away
   by beauty of the night.

A hush.
No sound.
The night slept silently beneath its silken coverlet.
The velvet drapes of midnight were pulled across the sky.
No light.
The trees and hills were blackened silhouettes against
   the blacker sky.
The streetlamp threw its timid circle scarcely twenty feet
   into the night.
All was still.
But dancing, frollicking, drifting through the muffled
   indigo
Were heaven's sparkling diamonds,
Their brilliance glistening against the velvet sky.

A hush.
No sound.
All still, but heaven's diamonds
Drifting across the midnight sky.

EUGENE HOLLAHAN

Vermeer's Window

In a silent night
She closed the cat outside
Framed in a pane of glass
Like a white secret thought.
Her melodic throat
Invited me to speak
Out of my lonely tent.
In a tangled wood
A complicated peace.

The weight of my embrace
Extracted from her throat
The golden drops of air
That raised the golden hair
About the white cat's face.
Mouth to mouth we blew
Our souls into our lungs.
We summoned from the woods
Every banished cat
That stalked inside our blood.

The cat's golden face
Glowed outside the glass
As if to supervise
Our windy enterprise.

Zeno Eyes Joyce the Streetwalker

Where the light breaks the blood
Thickens.   The knees flex   the feet
Rise in prayer   flower   flow through

Trieste's Giardino Pubblico.   That body
For once   for the nonce!   free   not
Tied to the white   sheets   the

Black marks   the sins   the
Sense!   Seeking   its father's face   his
Grace.   All things that break

Light mere   diversions.   Springtime!   May
That body meet good   men   and good
Men only in its   playful   its

Sporting walk.
May no halfway measures halt those
Joyful   steps   that cross this   park

Never   pray God!   never to reach a
Goal.   Never to pass from my loving   my greedy
My delaying

Eye.

B. LANCE LEVENS, JR.

A Gifted Child

Mrs. Valenti was depressed, and she didn't know why.

"David," she would say to her husband, a professional psychologist, "I am extremely depressed. David, are you listening?"

Usually David was not listening. When he was, his steelrimmed glasses would surface from behind the Journal of Psycho-something-or-other and his crocodile eyes would find his wife. He would say, "Val, I understand your feelings."

"Je-e-e-sus, David, you really are a trip. You know what I mean. Honestly, here I am cooped up in this redneck roadstop about to go bananas with a warped kid . . . I mean, really warped . . . and you 'understand my feelings . . .'"

The redneck roadstop was Clio, Georgia, population 25,000, give or take the number in the county mental health facility where her husband had been trasferred a year earlier. When Mrs. Valenti thought of Clio, she saw the bleached red-brick courthouse surrounded by mud-flecked pickup trucks. It was flat, hot, and muggy.

The kid was her son Ronald. As if it weren't enough that the mosquitoes were coming back for seconds on her neck and arms, or that people in town gawked at her when she said 'Schenectady,' on top of that, just that morning Ronald had folded their insurance papers into airplanes and sailed them out of the third-floor window into the yard across the alley where a bevy of Negro children was playing.

Ronald had reminded her of a monk when she caught him at the window ledge. Leaning out in his white denim housecoat, he had muttered something about an 'uneven glide.' She had explained patiently why the papers were not to be touched. Ronald had wrinkled his nose and pushed up his bi-focals to look at his calculator.

"I don't see why you wanna k-e-e-p 'em," he said. "Mutual's dropped twenty points on the market since Christmas."

By the time Mrs. Valenti had recovered the papers, the Rock of Gibralter had been scribbled over in yellow and black crayon with Picasso-like roosters. A massive black woman had gathered the papers while swatting the children with her open palm. Mrs. Valenti had protested, holding her hands over her mouth, as if she were horrified: "My God!" she yelled, "they're only babies! Don't kill them!"

The woman had not risen, but without looking, had thrust the papers toward Mrs. Valenti. "Heah . . . you want these im-paw-tunt papuhs or doan't you?"

David explained to Ronald that he had behaved 'inappropriately.'

Mrs. Valenti considered herself to be an intelligent woman, yet she was unable to control her own son while the Negro woman, who was probably illiterate, was doing the job with the back of her hand. But she already knew her husband's answer: David was very non-violent.

"Research has clearly proven . . ." he would begin, tapping his pipe bowl into the ashtray, or "One must remember that the average American child . . ." and clasp the back of his head in his leatherette reclining chair. Then she could see the black stitching on his gray elbow pads—her stitching!

Lately she had begun to worry over the prospect of an adult Ronald. His toys frightened her even now: space-age, geometric shapes in electric-colored plastic. Rollo the Robot that Ronald imitated by goose-stepping through the kitchen with his teeth clenched, spouting in monotone, made her flesh crawl. For consolation, she cloistered herself in the cool, pine-panelled den of their newly-restored old house and stuffed herself with chocolates.

At mid-day in Clio she could sit in the bay window and see through the tunnel formed by elms and oaks over their street all the way to the town square, blazing in the August heat. Across the street, a row of white, high-backed wicker rockers was usually pumping like a combustion engine, and it seemed to her that the occupants were always staring at her. One morning, browsing through a magazine on psychodietetics, she came across an uncanny article. It seemed to explain why she was having so much trouble with Ronald. She became so engrossed that she gobbled up the entire box of chocolates, including the pieces of foil. Above the article was the picture of a prominent New York psychiatrist in horn-rimmed glasses seeming to be falling on his face.

"Anger," the author said, "is the cause of depression. If you are depressed, there is someone you should be hating . . ."

She examined herself in the full-length mirror. Who did she hate? Jesus, who didn't she hate lately? When she looked at the weight she had gained, she reminded herself of a bowling pin. She had thought wearing her hair in braids would make her look younger; it was the style back in New York. Instead, she looked like a middle-age woman made up for the Wizard of Oz. Mrs. Valenti was thirty-five years of age. The black and grey-streaked braids hung down the front of her peppermint-striped polo shirt all the way to her faded jeans. Her broad cheery face was marred by wrinkles fanning out from the corners of her eyes.

She switched on a soap opera to think and get in touch with herself. The black woman kept popping into her mind. What a sense of power! She pounded her fist for several minutes, daydreaming about this. She was so absorbed in this delicious prospect that she didn't hear the wind whipping across the porch and the shutters banging.

She thought of the house. She had done it all and was proud. Mr. high-and-mighty David, the shrink, had done nothing but sniff around like a pig and complain about the paint fumes. She could still see him standing over her with that disgusted look of his, pointing to paint flecks on his tweed coat while she scrubbed the parquet. She grew drowsy as the TV light washed over her face, wave after wave, striping and speckling it.

A thunderclap startled her out of her reverie. Giving a grunt, she rolled her eyes and bestirred herself and walked to the floor-length window. This unreal heat! She felt like a sack of cement. Beneath the polo shirt, her skin was drenched. Elms and oaks that lined the street were bending in the wind. Another thunderclap faded erratically. In the North, on days like this she had loved to dawdle by the window when Ronald had been a baby. His tiny hand would find her nose and pinch it, or toy with the pin at the top of her bra. What had happened? How had she lost that tenderness? She pressed her face against the cool pane and told herself there was no wishing back the past.

Leaves swirled around in the gutters and rose and darted off in different directions like a flame. She imagined that the black family would be sitting on their porch, the six children waiting to splash through the puddles in the street and the mother behind them rocking furiously and fanning herself. Suddenly she realized why she felt so angry. Her right to punish her own son, her right as his mother, had been taken away. It had begun with David's ridiculous 'reinforcement precept,' whatever that was, all mixed up with candy, M & M's. The moment she had permitted Ronald to become enslaved to candy as a reward for good behavior was the moment she had handed over her rights. She wiped the sweat from her face and made an imprint of her hand on the window pane. Was the black woman's hand larger?

That night they ate on the porch. David was sitting with his sandaled feet propped on the rail, smoking his pipe. It seemed to her as she stooped and served—David was very particular—that all her anger from the afternoon had faded. Fireflies were weaving arabesques over the oleander. They seemed to sedate her as she ate. She waited for a long while before she spoke.

"David, I intend to punish Ronald physically the next time something like the insurance papers happens."

David took his nose out of the brandy snifter. Above his Hun-like moustache, his nostrils flared.

"Val, you know how I feel about . . ."

"Goddamnit, David, I've had it. By now I don't care how you feel. You don't have to live with him all day. I do." She was leaning against the rail, emphasizing her points by pounding her cigarette into an ashtray made of colored mosaic tiles. Oh how tired she was of David's academic clap-trap! 'An operational definition of intelligence,' 'learning threshhold,' 'stroking,' 'the love and withholding-of-love continuum . . .!' Clap-trap!

She began to gather up the dishes.

The next day in the hardware store she was looking over wire for her flower bed. The aroma of the corn feed and the neatness of the aisles and shelves she found soothing. The solicitous owner bounced around her industriously, talking out of the side of his mouth. When he squatted to arrange the wire for a mock garden setting, she saw the mole near the front of his scalp.

"I use this for my sweet potato bed . . ."

But Mrs. Valenti wasn't paying attention. The store was abustle. A large-framed woman with pink curlers in her hair was hauling a sack of feed into the store. The sleeves of her red-and-black checkered shirt were rolled up to her elbows, the hemline of her loose-fitting skirt dipped unevenly, and the scowl on her face made it plain that she was here to make a scene. Just outside, a skinny, barefooted boy in an undershirt and jeans was hoisting another sack out of the back of a blue pickup truck parked at the curb. "Maw!" he was yelling. "Wait, Maw . . .!"

"Dat's Mizz Creasy and her boy Wadley," a voice said from somewhere.

"Dis feed is rotten!" the woman yelled across the store.

The owner dispatched a helper to handle Mrs. Creasy. He continued to bob around Mrs. Valenti exclaiming all the while about Mrs. Creasy's temper what with her husband in jail and the kids always running loose and she always smelled like her goats and left that stink wherever she went. To Mrs. Valenti, Mrs. Creasy seemed to come from another world. The woman's face was grimy, leathery, deeply creased; she had no teeth and worked her lips back and forth, in and out, as if her mouth were filled with marbles. Mrs. Valenti guessed her age to be about fifty; the boy, nine or ten, about Ronald's age, although his sun-baked skin made him look older. She felt sorry for him watching him struggle with the sack of feed.

"How much do those sacks weigh?" she asked the owner.

"'Seventy-five pound," he said.

Mrs. Creasy was intently examining other sacks of feed when, all of a sudden, she looked up and yelled at the top of her lungs: "Where's dat boy! Wadley! You git in here, Wadley . . .! The boy was laboring under the second sack of feed he was lugging into the store. "You lazy good-fer-nothin'! I'm gonna slap the livin' fire out of you!" And obediently, quietly, the boy went out to the pickup truck and struggled with yet another sack of feed.

Mrs. Valenti was dumbstruck. No back talk, no leers, no temper display from the boy: just obedience. She wondered then how far the woman had gone in disciplining or punishing the boy. Did she beat him? Did she really slap the fire out of him?

When Mrs. Valenti got home, Ronald was sprawled on the porch swing with a stack of comic books beside him.

"You're late," was his greeting. "It's already past lunch time."

"Well, I'm sorry, your little Lordship."

"I've got Astronomy Club at 1:30 today. Fix me something."

The midday cicadas were droning like buzz saws. She made a baloney sandwich for Ronald and watched cooly as he stripped the crusts from the bread and aquired a cresent of Kool-Aid blue around his upper lip. When he bounded out to go to his club meeting, she stared, in a rage, at the curled brown crusts.

The next morning, on the porch, Ronald had wired a pair of frog legs—where obtained, she knew not—to a 12 V battery and watched with glee as they alternately leapt to tautness and eased back limply into peace at his manipulation of the wires. She realized finally that for the last few minutes, watching him from the den window, she had been tightening her whole body, then relaxing, then tightening. She would divert him. She wanted to get out of the house anyway. She prepared some peanut-butter sandwiches, took a bag of M & M's from a hidden place, and filled a cooler with cans of coke.

"Why do we have to go now?" Ronald whined.

"Mommy wants to catch some sun."

"What kind of jelly?"

"Grape. Space Ranger's favorite . . ."

"We had grape last time. Anyway, Space Ranger copped out when he married Krypton Woman."

As they walked along the elm-shaded sidewalk to the courthouse park, she tried to imagine how Mrs. Creasy would have reacted to such a reply. Ronald ran ahead and tried to shake, or he pounded on, every parking meter along the way.

Once on the courthouse square, Mrs. Valenti unfurled the picnic blanket and set the cooler and lunch-box down gingerly. The grass all around was mottled by the bright August sunlight filtering through magnolia trees and centuries-old, moss-hung oaks. Squirrels scampered here and there, and pigeons, strutting and cooing, eyed her expectantly. Ronald gathered some pebbles from around the edges of the blanket, worked them around in his fist for a few moments, then hurled them at the pigeons. The insatiable birds lifted into the air a few feet but quickly alighted again as near to the lunch-box as they dared.

"Ronald . . .!"

Ronald ignored her, gathered more stones, and bombarded the pigeons again.

She felt like a coiled spring, but determined not to let Ronald see her angry. By now, perspiration was dripping from the tip of her

212

nose. As she brought her forearm up to blot it away, Ronald thrust an ice-cube against her face, causing her to topple backwards. She righted herself slowly. The M & M's . . . No! Damn the M & M's. . . .!

Ronald was peeling the crusts away from his sandwich, and doing so very slowly. Damn it! Was he watching her and tormenting her deliberately?

Now he threw the sandwich down, rolled over onto his stomach, and began to punch the keyboard of his calculator.

"Aren't you going to finish your sandwich?"

"If that's all there is to eat, I'm not hungry."

Mrs. Valenti realized that someone was standing just to the back of her. She craned her neck around. It was the son of the toothless woman she had seen in the hardware store. What was her name . . .? And the boy . . Wadley; that was it, Wadley. Uneasy, barefooted, the boy shifted back and forth with both hands jammed into the pockets of his jeans.

"My momma wants ta' know if you got any scraps," he said.

Mrs. Valenti perkily got up onto her knees.

"Gee . . . well, I'll just take a minute and see. Where is your mommy?"

The boy pointed a skinny finger in the direction of a clump of azalea shrubs on the other side of the square. Mrs. Creasy was sitting on a cement bench feeding pigeons from a brown paper sack held between her knees. The boy looked at Ronald, and Mrs. Valenti thought she detected something of longing in the small blue eyes. Why, what it was was the calculator. She realized that this little country boy had never seen one before. He had probably never seen a Rollo the Robot either.

"Tell your momma I'll send something over in a minute," she said, and as if she had given a command to a well-trained dog, obediently the boy trotted away toward his mother.

It seemed to Mrs. Valenti that the day had turned into a steam bath. The ice had melted in the cooler leaving a single coke can afloat in what was now tepid water. She got the scraps together. Rather than invite a leer or sass from Ronald, she decided to run the little errand herself, but she wondered what would happen if she said, "Ronald, take these scraps to Mrs. Creasy or I'll slap the living fire out of you."

"Where are you going?"

Why did that child never address her as 'mother?' For that matter, he rarely addressed his father as 'dad' or 'daddy.' It was downright disrespectful, truly.

"Heah, chic chic; heah, chic chic . . ." The country woman was calling the pigeons. When Mrs. Valenti handed the scraps to her, she smiled her toothless smile and said, "'Preeshate it. 'Tank you, tank you . . ." And the boy intoned, "Tank you, tank you . . ."

It seemed that she had scarcely settled on the blanket beside Ronald when Mrs. Creasy and her son approached. "My boy wants a cold coke. Can you spare one?" She was holding the boy firmly by his bicep, as if she were expecting him to bolt away any moment. Then she spotted the water-filled cooler. "Yo' ice gone?" She spun the boy around and told him he would have to go to the drugstore. Ronald didn't even look up, but continued to punch at his calculator.

Mrs. Valenti heard herself saying, "Ronald, I'd like a cold coke, too. Go with ah . . . your new friend, ah . . . Wadley here. . . ."

"Do I have to?"

"Yes, you have to. Now come on, get up."

She fished in her purse for some change, and Ronald did not budge.

"Ronald!"

"Do I have to?"

"Ronald . . ."

"Why don't you . . .?

The coiled spring that had been in Mrs. Valenti all day finally snapped. She grabbed her son by the wrist, and amazed at her strength, for a moment dangled him in mid air like a rag-doll. A bitter smile came to her lips as she stared into Ronald's wild eyes. For an instant, she saw David, too. Clap-trap! Something inside said 'now,' and she slapped her son for the first time. Ronald's head shot back, his eyes flew wide open, tearing from the physical pain of the slap.

The country woman smiled lewdly.

"I told you, Ronald, that I wanted a coke. Now march over there and get me one!"

Inside Mrs. Valenti was fear covered over with ecstasy, bubbling up and up. She felt very good.

The country boy reached for Ronald who was still clutching his calculator but flailing his arms and sputtering. The two departed, and Mrs. Valenti was sure she heard the country boy say 'Shit on 'em' under his breath to Ronald.

Mrs. Creasy patted her on the arm. "You laid one on 'im then, didn't you!" she said. "I gots to swat mine two or 'tree times a day ta keep 'im in line. 'Got so used to it, I didn't even sting 'im. Now I got a razor strap . . ." The violence had caused the country woman to feel a kinship with Mrs. Valenti. She moved closer. "Want some crackerjack? It's good 'n sweet?"

Mrs. Valenti seemed not to hear. The ecstasy was already dissolving. She did not feel good. Her chest hurt. The shimmering heat of the day pressed against her whole being. More to herself than to the woman, she said softly, "Oh, I don't know . . ."

"What don't you know?" the woman said. "You don't know if you shoulda popped him?"

The woman bent over and put her brown bag on the ground. As she rose, she rolled up a sleeve of her frumpy dress to reveal an ugly, salmon-colored scar zigzagging from her elbow to her shoulder.

"What happened?" Mrs. Valenti asked, eyes full of horror.

"Dat's what dat lil' devil done with a butcher knife one night."

A scream pierced the air. The woman turned this way and that, uncertain, at first, of the direction from which it came. In the next moment they realized that it had come from the drugstore, which was about a half block away. "Oh, my God . . ." Mrs. Valenti screamed.

Ronald was lying on his back outside the drugstore. Across his forehead was a gash the shape of a butterbean hull. A crowd began to gather, but Mrs. Valenti's line of vision to the intersection at the edge of the square was unimpeded. There, crossing the street, was the country boy holding Ronald's calculator in his hand. As the passing drivers slowed and gawked, he held it out away from his body and admired it.

The White Perch

He whips amid the weed in even strokes,
Undulatory runner in the gloom.
Refracted glitter of the moonlight cloaks
Him in such a sheen he seems to plume
Himself in sewing shilly-shally sedge.
A quivering emanation seems to trail
Him on the sediment, as if a pledge,
The moon's fidelity. His tenuous tail
Whose gossamer is twisting in a shy
Swish, shuttling through the underwater fern,
Intimity, has interwoven sky
Within the skeins that sigh and yearn.
Then, he leaps up toward a fly, cleaves
The moon into a thousand sparkling leaves.

The River Washing

When my granny persuaded my grandfather Fred
To toss away his bottle and let
Himself be washed in the blood once more
(He gathered dust quickly after the washings),
Setting aside his argument—
His randy contempt for the ministry—
Like a regal liner leaving the shore
He hiked his britches, proud to be seen
Stamping out sin in such company,
And trilled until the scuppernong hollow
Rang in a sacred refrain . . .
Which he whistled in route to his sour mash store.

B. LANCE LEVENS, JR.

Divine Laughter

Your humor is too easily forgotten,
Lord. I know you chuckle, but so many
Of your sutlers don't. Break us up; any
Brooder in the pews—let him be undone

By joy and join with Miriam in dancing.
Douse our bowed heads with showers full of divine
Grins. Green our gray until our wise ones are prancing
Down the aisles to queue up in your comic line.

Point out the mirth of peccadilloes. Break
The spell. Regale us with pure cosmic cackles.
Lift to the light our ground bound eyes. Make
More and still more mirth 'til gloom stirs our hackles.

And when once we're to enter in your gates:
Still another laugh, Lord, at dirt cheap rates.

Notes for a Conversion

I dreamt of the moon, a swollen, indifferent eye,
Draining bloody fingers that strangled me.
Bronze grasshoppers steamed on the horizon,
Humming to throw off human tyranny.

When we were young, there was no light.

Sweat-washed, I lay like the dew-dappled leaf.
Poe's pendulum drew near, swept my breast.
Tongues, hound-tendrils, wound around my toes,
Turned to fire and singed me for a test.

Only the heart's conducive roar.

The roll call of dragons swelled beyond
My boyish skill at paining them. The cry
Of creatures dying in the wood—a king snake
Swallowing rabbits—this was my lullaby.

Is there one whose will is might?

Hero? Saint? To drive his anointed sword deep
Into the scaly breast, then stand aside
Gallantly as the writhing she-creature
Spits up human gobbets in a green tide?

Vision in the fire-laced door?

Years later, He took my salvaged heart in hand,
But not before He nudged me to the brink
And forced my eyes downward. "See," he said,
"At bottom it's your own, wrathful sink."

When we were young, there was no light,
Only the heart's conducive roar.
Then came He whose will is might,
Vision in the fire-laced door.

Fol de Nuit

Good evening, lays and gin-amen, this is flight
703 departing from the Midnight Blues.
Ahead, you will observe the Cosmic Bite.
On clear evenings you can see the ooze

From last night's passenger who just couldn't keep
From leaning out the window. While the beast smiles
We will serve your members gelée. A heap
Will be wandering at all times through the aisles.

Please, if you must use the facilities,
Do so quietly. Any undue agitation
Of the pilot could alarm his faculties
Which function poorly upon castration.

Oh, and just a word of caution concerning hope.
If at any time you should see blue,
Please shout (with decorum, of course). Our oscilloscope
Has banged his snout probing the Primal Goo.

Willie

Willie?
He smoke strange weed.
Send he eyes to 'de Dry Tortugas.
Make he lips go coo-coo.
Make he organs go organic.
Make he hips go bumpety-hump like
                    Xavier Coooo-gat.
Green weed make Willie a post man,
                    post he woman deep
                        into her jive-ass squiggly
                        where her red worm wiggles
                        and her squid goes ooooze.
Make Willie a bad ass.
Burn, flame, everything die:
    Dog blood, chicken blood, fox blood, cow blood
    blood from Tahiti mail ordered
    mammy blood
    little ol' lady blood
    and sweet innocent children blood
        blood of the most unintegrated
        or ever by the Labor Dept. squashed and kicked in the
        hacked over genitals rose

    will not satchify.

Come heaven,
Come Hell—quick—
And get poor Willie McTell,
    nice,
        a one-time choir boy.

B. LANCE LEVENS, JR.

A Truncated Sonnet on Impossible Love

When suns no longer bulge and sizzle,
When stars switch off and strike for better light,
When scholars shave their ibids to a pizzle,
When hoary saints are wasted on delight,

When vague ideas will bear one over seas,
When kidneys push, like Sisyphus, the stone,
When ichor flows from fresh lobotomies,
When muezzins proclaim in monotone,

When picky girls in nasal passageways
Sollicit lonely souls to sell advice,
When hawk-eyed fishes swoop the skies and raze
The sea of serpents, scaled and finny mice,

Then lovers will purely love
With hearts as pure as ice.

A Walk Down Lincoln Street

The children's eyes glaze as the gold car plows
Through their sea, leaving a wake of hate dreams
To slap against their salt-hoary brows.
But the candy store is near with creams,
Sucrose, their children's opiate, to still
An already budding desire to kill.

Dust whispers to the marigold
Of vengeance though a baby cups its bud.
Here, there is no rain. What the clods hold
Must be slake and nourished by the blood.
I stop for a cold soft drink, wonder why
The cashier razors me a brown-veined eye.

Trying to mimic air, I stroll along
The sidewalk, grinning till my lips are ripped.
A booze-gaseous beggar spits a gravelly song.
No one seems to bother that his brain's unzipped.
We're brothers, I say to myself. Late,
I'm learning now what is our common fate.

Back on the side of right, trim and so
Organized, the shoppers share a tale
Of tidy feelings. It enthralls. We know.
Harmony's bred by class. I check my mail,
Toss out the junk and wonder: who could need
A sweepstakes win? Is there no end to greed?

B. LANCE LEVENS, JR.

Catullus: XLV

Septimius and Acmen
In ardent clasp: "I would not love
Another, should you pass." he vows.
"I am prepared to show my love
Through all eternity. Like one
Arrayed with a thousand lives, alone
In deserts or in the jungle deep,
I'd stand before the lion dame
To illustrate fidelity."
At these oaths Cupid sneezed
His liking, both to left and right.
But Acmen, lifting light her brow,
Her pupils swimming with her sweet,
Her lips all bright with purple wine:
"Septimius, I'll kneel to you for life.
You're my only lord; may fires
Within me burn longer, more bright."
At these oaths, Cupid sneezed
His liking, both to left and right.
These love, love to be loved, start
With favorable auspices.
Wretched Septimius prefers
His Acmen to Britannia
And Syria; faithful Acmen diverts
Septimius with a light
Lustful proclivity.
Where have you seen such a lucky pair,
Venus in such prosperity?

Virgil: Eclogue X

Grant me, Arethusa, this last work,
Lines I needs must offer for my Gallus, yet
Not a word Lycoris would ever shirk.
Would any take offense that I have turned

These words to tune for Gallus? Then, begin,
Lest you grime yourself with briny seas
When you dive under Sicily's salt and fin.
Let's sing of Gallus, how his love has brought

Him pain. The goats with their flat faces will crop
The gentle brakes. We chant to no deaf ears.
The trees will heed our notes, toss back every stop,
When Gallus with unworthy tears pined

You Naiads, where were you, in what grove or glade?
Parnassus, Pindus, Aganippe—
For none would you tarry. Tamarisks and laurels swayed,
Grieving. Maenalus with his cone cap

Wept at the sight of Gallus underneath
A solitary crag. The gelid stones
In the Lycaeus cried. From the heath
Unfettered by our human shame the flocks

Drew round (divine poet, do not feel shame
Because of sheep: beautiful Adonis,
He, too, took flocks to water); shepherds came,
Their swineherds ambling easily after;

Menalcus came, too, from a mast where he'd soaked
A winter—each with a question for you:
"What love is this of yours? What provoked
This madness, Gallus?" asked Apollo.

"Lycoris treads behind another man.
Your love follows the brutish, frozen camps."
Silvanus, garlands mock-genteel, shook a fan
Of glowing fennel, of tall lillies.

The god of Arcady, Pan, came, his dress
Vermillioned with elderberry. He said:
"Is there no term to tears? Love could care less.
Nor do painfilled eyes pacify that god,

Nor does a brook the grass; nor is the bee
Filled by the clover, nor the goat his leaf."
But Gallus, downcast, said: "Folk of Arcady,
These things you'll sing upon your mountains

For you're the masters at it, only you.
Oh, how softly my bones will rest at last
On the day that your reed-pipes endue
My loves with song. If only I'd been born

As one of you, a shepherd to tend your fold
Or a dresser of your early vine. I'm sure
If Phyllis or Amyntas were there to hold,
Whatever my madcap state (What then,

If Amyntas is a darker shade?
Hyancinths are dark, violets, too.)
We'd while away in a willow cascade
Beneath a lazy vine. Amyntas would sing,

Phyllis weave a garland of colored bloom.
The spring-water, Lycoris, is cold here;
The fields soft; groves, too. Only time would consume
Us. But now mad war drives me spear-eyed

To pursue the enemy while you
Far from home (Can I really confide
In such a tale?) look on the Alps. Ah, harsh view,
The Rhenish ice and snow and you without me.

GEORGIA ON MY MIND

May the cold not freeze you; may the ice not tear
Your tender soles. I'll go and play my verses
Adapted to Chalcidean, air
Them on my Sicilian shepherd's reed-pipe.

Indeed, I do prefer to suffer here
In this wood, in these savage caves, to carve my love
On tender trees. When the saplings near
Their fulness, they extend my feelings to the stars.

Meanwhile, I'll roam Maenalus, hand in hand
With boisterous nymphs, or I'll bag the wild boar.
Hoar-frost will never freeze my howling band
Out of the passes on Parthenios.

I see myself now in the rocks and groves
Delighting to let fly a Cydonian shaft
As if such games could mend my madding love,
Or as if that god might move to soften.

Hamadryads, once again; songs, too,
No more will you enchant me. Farewell, you forests!
There is nothing our suffering can do.
The god won't change. Whether you draw from the Hebrus

In mid-winter a tooth-chilling drink
Or brave the sloshy Thracian snows; or when
The high bark of the elm begins to shrink
And you, beneath a July sky, are driving

A fold from Ethiopia—everything
Is quelled by love: we, too, will kneel to him.
For the poet to bring his verse and sing
Will be, gods, enough, while he sits and weaves

A canister. Now, Pierides, lift these rhymes
To highest worth for Gallus, Gallus for whom
My love grows faster than an elder climbs.
Rise. Shade for singers is a dark sign.

Shadows are noxious to a juniper.
Shadows even do injury to grain.
Homeward, my full flock, the evening star's astir.
Up, ladies, up, let's make our way towards home.

C. Baudelaire: The Cracked Bell

It's sweet and bitter on a winter's night
To hear beside the smoking, popping blaze
The distant memories rise and take flight
On chiming bells that penetrate the haze.

The happy-throated bell still vividly
Resounds in its grisly years, no impediment,
Unleashing its devout cry faithfully,
An old soldier rising in his tent.

My soul is cracked as well. When nights turn lead
And she would take the cold air and thread
It with her warm notes, often her song

Is the thick râle of a wounded man along
A lake of blood, lost in a mound of death,
Dying without a move with strained breath.

J. BRYANT STEELE

Blackberry Picking

Twenty-five feet on both sides of the road, my father always said. That's how much the government owns and any taxpayer has as much right as another to eat what grows there.

Mama would answer how it was unchristian to take what did not belong to you and then you would have to strain to hear her after that. The noisy Plymouth was never a match for Daddy's strident tenor, but Mama's voice always got vesper soft when she started talking about her religion. To make it worse, Daddy would race the unmuffled engine, daring Mama to make his car an altar. Mama would cross her arms and mutter out the window until the engine died down, then shout "praise God I'm a Christian" with the same fervency she generally used at prayer meeting.

Sometimes Daddy would tease Mama instead, saying something like, "You're a Christian second and a cook first. You'll start cooking soon as we get home, and won't allow me to have even a mouthful of what I helped pick."

But Mama didn't see how something could be both sacred and funny, so there was little rest from the arguing as we bumped up and down in the car, scouting for berries growing wild along the rights of way, while Mama struggled with her fundamental beliefs over the rightness and wrongness of it. Each excursion awaited its own judgment; if the Lord allowed us to get back safely to the house with the fruit then that was His sign He didn't consider it ill-gotten. That's why Mama pestered Daddy about gambling, his winnings were ill-gotten. Daddy told her once that if the Lord allowed him to win that was His sign of approval. Mama knelt right there in the kitchen and asked God to forgive her blasphemous husband.

Daddy ordinarily knew how much gainsay Mama could stand and he would stop short of a fight. The only real fights came when Mama would try earnestly to convert Daddy, to save his soul, as she put it. But they loved each other, and sometimes Daddy would trudge along with us to church just to keep peace.

It was good the Lord was gracious enough to allow us to pick wild berries. We depended on the dollars Mama could earn selling her jellies and preserves made from muscadines, plums, strawberries and, most often, the abundant blackberries. Daddy was a hard worker, but he didn't have a regular job. He could make some money playing cards. He could round up a card game as well as Mama could round up a prayer meeting. But Mama would not touch his winnings, so Daddy hired himself out as much as he could for common labor and odd jobs.

Whenever we spied what looked like good pickings, Daddy would pull the car over and the bickering would succumb to a sense of purpose. My sisters, Lotti and Betty, and I were supposed to help, but we always ate more than we put in the baskets, and after eating our fill we would play. Betty and I would chase each other with blackberries, fistfuls of them, and squash them on each other. The red Georgia dust would settle on our sweat-drenched bodies and mix with the blackberry juice, which left a dark stain hard to remove. Mama could not stand for us to be so filthy and periodically she would look up from her work and promise us a scrubbing and a whipping when we got home. We usually avoided the whipping.

One day a Negro family came by in a car even more dilapidated than our own. The car slowed. They were berry pickers, too. After a long look, maybe figuring to come back later, they started off again.

"Hey, come on down. There's plenty here."

"Amos!"

"There is. Come on, we've almost filled up anyhow. Shame to let all these berries go to waste."

"Amos, those are colored people. Too late. Here they come. Children, behave. We'll be finished soon."

They left the car on the other side of the road and brought their baskets. There were four children, two boys and two girls. Daddy said howdy to the parents, they said it to him, and they started picking, keeping a distance between us. I watched, behaving, until my curiosity won. I walked up to the oldest boy, about my size. No one else was paying attention. I thought it would be great to play with someone my size and strength, someone who saw life through a boy's eyes. I was suddenly very tired of my little sisters.

But I didn't know what to say as we stood there. I had a handful of blackberries I'd intended for Betty. I smeared them across his cheek. He did not move or resist. I grinned to show it was sport. He stuck out his tongue.

I would have expected that from Betty, but he was supposed to be equal to the game, to spit on me or try to wrestle me into the dirt. Not stick out his tongue like a girl. I could have fixed him quick, could have bloodied his nose, but that would have just made trouble for me. I thought of another way to get even.

"Daddy, that boy has stuck his tongue out at me."

The boy's mother heard me. She grabbed him by the arm, slung him out in front of her and spanked him hard three times. He started crying and she told him to quiet down or she would spank him again. She and her husband then turned their backs to us.

Daddy had not answered me. I felt better now that the boy had been spanked, but I wanted my father to at least say something. I'd sensed we had that right. So I told him again the boy had stuck out his tongue at me.

"He's just trying to be friends."

"That's a funny way to be friends."

"Better than your way." He'd seen the blackberry juice. And he was taking their side. I stomped my bare foot in the dust and raised my voice at him.

"He stuck his tongue out at me!"

"Then stick yours out at him," Mama answered. That, at least, was some response, and it had Mama's approval. I turned back to the other family. My foe stared through teary eyes, biting his lower lip to keep from crying and bringing on more punishment. I planted my feet and stuck out my tongue as far as it would go. His brother and sisters laughed, so I did, too. I guessed the fight was over and stepped forward thinking we might play after all. I stopped when I looked at him. His eyes still fixed on me. His tears had left shiny trails on his dusty face. The blackberry juice had run down to his chin, but it was beginning to dry. His chest and shoulders trembled from wanting to cry.

My temper had cooled and there was a sudden swirl in my mind that was upsetting things I had commonly accepted, things I had taken in and believed were all the doctrine I would need as a boy and a man. My soul had been saved two years before, when Mama and our preacher had decided I was old enough to learn about Jesus, and out of conscience and out of fear I had decided that when I grew up I would not play cards and I would trust God's judgment whenever I picked berries, because Mama had made me want to do right things and not wrong. But now wrong was a new word to me and it had nothing to do with picking berries or betting money on cards. Those were just charades to resist.

Though he was about my age, I realized as I looked at him that he knew things I didn't yet because the question that had just come to me he of course had asked himself long ago, and as I was struggling to reconcile it he had known for a long time the answer was that there was no divine reason.

I wondered how all the betrayal must have hurt him. He would realize one day, as I would, that his mother had spanked him to protect him, because she didn't know who or what we were. But now, with blackberry juice caked on his face, he could not understand why he had to be the sinner. He could not retaliate. He could not pout or throw a tantrum. He could only bite his lip and tremble. His brother and sisters had laughed at him, his mother and father had turned their backs, and he had no recourse. No one has ever hated me the way he did, and I stood facing him, my hands behind my back and my head hung, letting him.

Neither of us moved until it was time for my family to leave. Mama and Daddy were arguing quietly. I could not hear everything, but they were arguing because Daddy had invited the black family to pick berries with us. When Daddy started the car in the middle of her sentence, Mama raised her voice and, grabbing the door, slammed it hard for emphasis.

Lotti screamed. The door had slammed on her hand. Confusion suddenly replaced the anger. Mama grabbed Lotti and held her tightly. Then Mama began screaming and Lotti screamed louder. There was blood on Mama's dress. I got out of the car and saw Lotti's hand. I felt dizzy and began vomiting. I leaned against the car and saw Betty inside with her eyes closed. I thought it was lucky for her she could sleep. I did not know until later she had fainted. No one could have slept through those screams.

Daddy was trying to take Lotti but Mama would not let go. He slapped Mama but she kept screaming and holding Lotti. I think all the black children were crying or yelling. The black man was spitting tobacco juice into his wife's hands. She was working her hands together and he was spitting in them. It should have been curious, but I accepted everything as sensible, the way you do in a dream.

Lotti got quiet. Daddy kept trying to take her away from Mama but Mama kept screaming and refused to let go. I was thinking Lotti was dead when the black woman ran up and held out her hands. She was holding mud. That's why he had been spitting into her hands, they were turning dirt into mud. Mama stopped screaming and looked at the offering.

"It'll stop the bleeding."

Mama nodded. They began applying the mud to Lotti's hand. I remember my granny once said that a mud poultice was good to stop bleeding.

Daddy told me later that mothers have a kindred spirit that overcomes unnatural barriers and that's why Mama would listen to a stranger and not her husband.

The bleeding stopped and we left for the hospital. It was thirty miles away and night had fallen by the time we got there. It was the first time I had been in a hospital. I always associate with that time whenever I'm in one and I dread even visiting in them.

Lotti was in the emergency room a long time. Mama kept Betty and me with her on an uncomfortable bench. Daddy sat outside smoking. After a time, I went out to sit with him. When he turned to look at me the lights glimmered on his face and showed me his grief. I told him Lotti was going to be all right and he shouldn't worry. He smiled at me. I had helped him, and that made me feel good.

"You sure are filthy. Mama will be scrubbing on you for a long time."

"We ought to let Mama scrub all the children. She'd scrub all our skins off and nobody could tell if we were black or white."

"Either that or put the bunch of you in a blackberry patch and after a time you'd all be covered in dust and juice and nobody could tell the difference."

I laughed. Then I put my face in his shirt and cried. After that, I was closer to him than Mama wanted me to be.

Practically everything I learned about being a man he taught me. guess he had wondered, in my first few years, if he was ever going to have that chance. He taught me how to deal poker, all the time urging me not to become a gambler. But mostly I learned from listening to him. He liked to talk about why he did things the way he did, and what his hopes were. He never told me what to think or instructed me on what was right or wrong. He did not want me to be like him, but I'm sure he hoped that when I was a man people would see some of him in me. I think the main thing he taught me was to try to go my own way and be understanding, and that understanding takes a lot of tolerance.

I haven't seen him since Mama's funeral. I took a job in Atlanta last year and before I ever went back home to visit Mama died. I told Daddy then that I would be back to see him in June but when I returned he was gone. Folks say that after the funeral he put all his clothes in the car and drove off. They haven't seen him since. Betty and I have tried to locate him, but I don't think he wants to be found.

NANCY MAXWELL GOLDBERG

Yam ha Melah (Salt Sea)

The Dead Sea is not dead:
Valuable minerals can be
    removed;
Bodies can float amidst
pillars worthy of a woman
    turned to salt;
(The cost was high for that
    last look
But immortality shows its
face in vaunting ways).

The Dead Sea is not dead:
Resorts abound along its
    shores
And waters cure an arthritic
For that fraction of a second
    that understands ecstasy.
The sun hurts, and heats, and
    soothes
And bakes the salted beach
Which alienates curious human
    feet,
But does not allay its savage
assault on virgin flesh.

There is no relief from sun
And salt, lacing sea and air,
But the Dead Sea is not dead;
The Dead Sea awaits the Millenium.

Now the forest presents bouquets

Now the forest presents bouquets of turning
  leaves,
Heavy with rain they project their vulnerability
  to the changing season.
The trees, drooping from the fatigue of a hot
  Georgia summer,
Have informed the birds they can no longer
Make a home among them.
But the squirrels frivolously ignored the
  poignancy of the moment,
As they leap from limb to limb providing a
Clamourous wake to salute the death of summer.

MICHAEL MATTHEWS

Pay Me

Bill Monroe stepped outside into the warm, breezeless night. Sunset Boulevard was crowded. The cars moved lazily along, embarked on their destinations to nowhere. He lit a cigarette, a Winston, and continued walking, easily, quietly.

The whores were out in full force; and he watched them conspicuously, gaudily, patrol their respective "turfs." Why was it, he wondered, that they always looked as if they were heading to a costume ball? There was blond hair, blue hair, orange hair, and seemingly every other color perched atop their garrish outfits; outfits pinching white skin, black skin, yellow skin, brown skin. It was enough to make any sane person nauseous. And Bill Monroe was a sane person.

He took a long drag, ashed his smoke, and cocked his head from side to side. He looked up at the sky. The view rewound his brain to the time when he was a kid going to the planetarium on a Saturday afternoon with his mom. It seemed such a wondrous, immense configuration then as it hovered above, embedded in a vast blue backdrop. He remembered having to tilt his head way back, so far that his mouth plopped open, to take it all in. The endless panorama spread before him now seemed equally as large but somehow less structured, more chaotic; as if the Lord had taken a bucket of those glistening, white pindots and merely dumped them into a huge, gooey vat, causing them to stick where they now sparkled.

"You want a date, honey?"

He turned to the sound, focused, and flicked his stub into the street. She came closer. She was tall, about 5', 11", with smooth, copper-colored skin. Her hair was shoulder-length, thick brown, and parted in the middle. She was very pretty. It disgusted him even more.

"My name's Jamba. You lookin' for a date?" Her accent was clipped yet lilting. He could tell she was from the Caribbean. A struggling model he guessed.

"Oh . . . I don't know." He was purposefully laconic.

"I'm in the Stardust; right over there. Come on." She smiled and lightly grabbed his left forearm. He wanted to laugh but concentrated on the ground instead. They walked on in silence.

241

"I'm right in here." He found her eagerness rather disconcerting, as if she were leading him into a trap. But it didn't really bother him. He could take care of himself. Still, as she opened the navy blue door wearing a gold 9, he looked to each side before entering.

It was a typical motel room, cheap but clean. A radio was turned on. It was tuned in to a "mellow rock" station, or some such bullshit. On the farthest of the two beds a small Oriental woman sat filing her nails.

"Say hello, Ann."

She did. Bill nodded and smiled faintly.

"What's your name?" the shorter lady asked.

"Oh, it doesn't really matter, does it?"

Both ladies forced a laugh. The Amazon shut the door and walked to the desk centered against the wall. She rummaged in her large, tan purse.

"Cigarette?" she asked.

"Yeah. Thanks."

The smoke she handed him was long and thin. He read the label. Virginia Slims. He wanted to vomit. Instead he reached for a book of matches extolling the virtues of staying at the Stardust, lit up, then handed them to Jamba. She sauntered over to the open bed and laid down gracefully. She cocked her right arm behind her head. Ann placed her file on the nightstand and looked up.

Jamba spoke: "What are you lookin' for tonight?"

"What do you do?"

"Whatever you want . . ."

"If you've got the money," Ann blurted in. The two women exchanged knowing glances and laughed.

"Is that right?" Bill smiled while placing his smoke in the tray.

"Kinda like a candy store, eh?"

"Yeah," Jamba said while taking her arm down and flickering her cigarette.

"Well . . .," he crossed his arms and perched on top of the desk chair.

"Let's see what you got, ladies."

Immediately Ann pulled off her top, exposing firm purple-dotted breasts. Her cut-off shorts quickly followed. Then she laid down with her hands bent back under the pillow. It made a pretty picture.

Jamba was more cautious. "Let's see the green, man."

"Sure." He reached for his wallet and pulled out a fifty. He tossed it on her bed. She saw the denomination, put out her cigarette, stood up, and disrobed. He moved to the side of the bed and sat on the edge. Jamba laid back down.

"Nice," he soothed. He began stroking her right calf. Ann sat up expectantly.

"Does the phone work?" he asked.

"It should," Jamba said.

"Good."

He reached for it and felt for the cord. Then he yanked it free from the wall.

"What did you do that for?"

He smiled sardonically. "I guess I don't want to be disturbed."

Quickly he noosed Jamba's neck and pulled it tight, hard. She choked a response. Her hands jerked to the source of the pain. Her protruding nipples hardened. Ann couldn't believe what she was seeing. She pounced on him shouting, "Stop! Stop, you asshole! You're hurting her!" He shoved an elbow into her ribs. The force knocked her to the floor. Then he resumed his torture, viciously pinching the cord tighter, usurping all of Jamba's life-force. Her body went limp a few seconds later; her head listed to one side; her fingers released their clutching and opened, slowly, as if they were flowers blooming. Then he wheeled around, jammed a hand into his pocket, and found his stiletto. He unearthed it, heard the cold, sure click, and pointed it toward the ceiling. He dangled it between his fingers. By that time Ann had stumbled to her feet holding her side. Then she saw what he was wielding. She backed up slowly. Her eyes enlarged. Bill walked toward her. Jamba's lifeless left arm flopped off the bed.

Ann's voice was shaky. "Go away . . . Leave me alone . . . Plea—"

He thrust his knife into her gut. She was momentarily impaled against the wall; then she slumped to the floor. He reached for her cut-offs lying on the bed and wiped the weapon clean in one motion. Before turning the doorknob he stashed the bill in his shirt pocket. Then he surveyed the carnage.

"Ignorant bitches," he muttered.

In the next instant he was out the door, leaving it ajar. He made his way to the main drag where he felt a small breeze blowing in from the coast. It felt good on his face.

He didn't run.

PHILLIP DEPOY

A Dream of Zebras

Night closed over the earth;
a beak closed over the seed

in the throat of a cuckoo
on a sleep-bent olive branch.

Rain pierced the deep green lake
with a thousand silver spears.

The cuckoo dreamed of zebras
in the crush of the dripping veldt,

and when it awoke
the zebra's back

was imitated by the lightning pressed
against the rain-black sky.

The Kingfisher's Book

An angle of the river fell
like an instrument of architects

exactly bisecting the rock
with water and sunlight

beside the purple kingfisher's
hole, dug in the empty bank.

On the rock in sunlight
stood the kingfisher

watching minnows glide
the watery line around his wing.

"They have nothing in their mathematics,"
said the old bird to the sky-white fishes,

"to compare with this chicanery."
Numberless fishes fell like figures

in the purple calculations
of an unseen, formless book.

VLADIMIR VOLKOFF

The White Pine Wardrobe

It was rectangular, rectilinear, new, clean, sturdy. Made of white pine too. Well designed, with shelves on one side, a closet on the other, and an elastic band for ties on the left door. Chromated balls for door knobs, a round lock, a flat key.

The perfect wardrobe—no neurosis, no history, unpretentious, and without skeletons or mystification.

Somehow it calmed me.

And Heavens knows I could have done with some calming.

I was in hiding at the time in a nondescript room, under a false name, in a new city with deadly perpendicular streets, respectable shop windows, and nice, neat citizens addicted to municipal showers and weekly movies. I hid and tried to forget.

I was beginning to do so. I no longer had nightmares. I no longer trembled when I saw my face in an unexpected mirror. And now and then I got a reassuring pleasure from the movies and showers.

Everything would perhaps have turned out well if it hadn't been for the white pine wardrobe, which had a single fault: even closed, its two doors fit together poorly and formed an angle just short of being straight.

One night I woke up. And since the moon was out, I could see, eyes wide open, that my white pine wardrobe was opening. So slow, so relentless. I raised up on an elbow . . .

"No . . . no."

The movement was scarcely perceptible. Neither does one see the hour hand move. And there was no mistaking it. The time would come when the two doors would be parted, and the viscera of the ripped open wardrobe would be unbared.

"No."

Spontaneous opening on my duds, borrowed suits, underclothes yet unaccustomed to my body, and variegated, pseudonymous ties. What would I do if these things took sides against me? (Things know every secret, of course.)

Already a crack was appearing between the two doors. Menacingly, they continued to lean forward, to unfold, and to open up like lips shut tight until then on some unutterable secret.

251

I don't know how I managed to put my bare feet on the cold floor and go close the doors again. Not very hopefully, however.

Back in bed, I saw that the wardrobe was starting to open again. Standing there in the white shadow, it smiled an inexpiable, vertical smile.

The next day I phoned headquarters:

"Lock me up, or I'll collapse."

And I added:

"Blame it on the wardrobe."

VLADIMIR VOLKOFF

Ministories of Life and Death

Juliette had fair hair and middle-aged middle-class parents. Robert had nothing but a small black moustache. So they were not allowed to be married.

As Robert was fond of reading about mishaps and misdemeanours, and Juliette entertained lovely ideas on the subject of love, they resolved to take a room in a dingy hotel and commit suicide.

But, as it soon appeared, there had been a misunderstanding.

Fondly Robert imagined they would kill each other in the morning. Not so Juliette: the evening was her choice. When they perceived they differed on that point, they indulged in some gnashing of teeth. He was called a cad; she a fool. She fled; he did not pursue. Six months later she was married to a bald notary.

When they came to murder the old general Duke von Hoherwald-Stalburg-Woltha, he was in bed and his valet told him:

"The door will hold one or two minutes. Your Grace can escape through the bathroom and take refuge on the floor below, in the flat of Your Grace's friend, the colonel von Edelstadt-Undsoweiter."

But the general's clothes were in the dressing-room, and the dressing-room down the passage, and the passage swarming with murderers; so it seemed the general would have to face the colonel in rather informal dress.

"No one has ever seen a Duke von Hoherwald-Stalburg-Woltha in his nightshirt and no one ever will," stated the old gentleman.

And let himself be knifed.

Obviously valets and murderers did not count.

Edmond was sixteen. He smoked a pipe and wished for two things in the world: to kiss the hand of a lady and to die immediately after. Tonight he wished it stronger than ever.

He was so engrossed in inventing a comedy of art with hand-kissing in it that he did not notice Jacquotte impatiently goading him on. When finally his lip had brushed against the tip of her longest nail, he went out, mad with joy.

Jacquotte's disappointment went unobserved. Edmond strode towards the sea. There was no point in surviving such happiness.

When he reached the end of the dam, he felt the manly desire to smoke one last pipe before jumping.

The smoking he punctually fulfilled; the jumping he forgot. And the morrow found him wondering about the feeling of a girl's cheek under a man's mouth.

Two identical old beaux, wearing identical silk hats, white ties and black capes, stood on the Alexandre III Bridge, looked at the black shining water, and exchanged memories of the times when they were both pleasant young rakes. And the blue-blooded one, who thought that the other had been an understanding husband, not a blind one, spoke thus:

"Well, after Isabelle, it must have been your charming wife, my dear fellow."

The dear fellow had no objection to that. But, sore at having been what he thought was a dupe, he immediately exclaimed—although he would never had dared lift his eyes up to a woman protected by a title (an authentic one by the way):

"The time when I assiduously frequented yours, my dear boy."

The old cynic—I mean the blue-blooded—strained his last forces and threw his companion into the Seine.

The great and big composer went on improvising on his Erard and, managing a subtle smile on his fat face, he spoke thus to the lovely singer who had no voice:

"Yes, my dear, there would be a part for you in my opera. I should of course expect you to become my mistress."

"Maestro, you have no manners," snapped she.

"Well, my wife then," said lazily the composer and played on.

He believed in getting things the easy expensive way whenever he could not get them the easy and cheap one.

So they were married and she made him happy and he never knew what had gone on that day in that pretty red-haired head of hers:

"His mistress? What wonderful luck! I need not trouble any more about my career. Still he should have stopped playing."—Maestro, you have no manners. "His wife? Well, I have always noticed gentlemen were rude to their wives."—Certainly, maestro; for better and for worse.

It happened at a small cafe in the rue Bonaparte where Beaux-Arts freshmen were being subjected to traditional ordeals by their elders. When Christophe's turns came to swallow the live gold fish, he seemed decidedly unwilling. They caught him, pushed him against the wall, opened his mouth, and one of them held the fish dangling by the tail.

Christophe took out a switchblade from his trousers pocket, stabbed a future genius two fingers under his left nipple, lifted the writhing fish from the floor and delicately replaced it in its bowl.

When examined about his motives, he explained he was an animal lover.

Jules as a being was extraordinary. Still he had to impress the fact upon a distrustful world. So he played truant, read forbidden novels, had his doubts about the reliability of God, composed verse at sixteen, married against the wish of his parents, was scrupulously unfaithful to his wife, and died as what is generally supposed to be a good Christian.

The air was soft and fragrant. Monsieur and Madame Pilpillou, such a sweet happy couple, followed a flowery path. They went to visit Monsieur and Madame Liliers, such a sweet happy couple too.

The gentlemen smoked fine cigars in the garden. The ladies went into the house to admire Mme Liliers's new vacuum-cleaner. Suddenly the husbands wanted to explain to each other what the deuce they were so happy about. Which they did, purely and coarsely. And the wives had the same inspiration; which they followed, daintily and dirtily. Soon the two couples were stripped of their most secret secrets.

The evening came. Mouths smiled. Hands shook hands. Goodbye, they said. It was farewell to somebody else. Somehow Monsieur and Madame Liliers, Monsieur and Madame Pilpillou were unhappy forever after.

Ernestine of the first floor was insignificant and a milliner. Oscar of the second was insignificant and a clerk. For him she varnished her nails; for her he brilliantined his hair. Every evening he came down to see her. They never entertained; they never even went to the movies.

Last January she died, and he died in February. They had genius those two, as Petrarch and his Laura.

VLADIMIR VOLKOFF

Lot's Lot

(Story from Genesis 18 and 19)

Characters:
Mr. Lot
Mrs. Lot   *55'ish*

Fernie
Lola   *their daughters, late teens*

Sam   *boyfriends of the girls,*
Tom   *late teens*

Af   *angels of destruction,*
Kezef   *30'ish in appearance*

They   *from 5 to 13 unisex*
                             dancers

Note:

Description of the set and indication of light effects can be disregarded in amateur productions. The setting, in that case, can consist of a rocking-chair, three entrances and a chalk line on the floor to separate "the porch" from "the ground". On the other hand the music and whatever costumes and props are indicated should be considered essential.

Set   *(see note above):*

The stage represents the porch of an old run down house. Slender Victorian columns upholding a gingerbread roof with Spanish moss hanging from it. Balustrade. Two or three steps in bad need of repair lead to the ground level which occupies the dowstage area, call "the street." A door upstage leads into "the house." An imaginary area on the actors' right is "downtown." An imaginary area on their left is "the country."

Lights off. A deafening rock style music explodes "downtown." Shrill, frenzied voices, hysterical quality, words impossible to distinguish. A few seconds of din. In mid-phrase, total silence.

257

1st VOICE (*backstage*)—Why d'you cut the music?
2nd VOICE (*backstage*)—They've got to hear the lines, don't they?
1st—But they've got to know what it's like downtown, don't they?
2nd—They know. You've put it loud enough.
1st—Still we've got to keep them in the right mood.

> *The music comes back, but much lower, and has dwindled back to nothing when it is time for the first speech. It will resume later, as indicated.*
>
> *Lights go slowly on on stage. Yellowish tint, appropriate for early sunset. In addition, revolving lights, disco style, red dominant, come from "downtown." For the present, they turn very slowly, and, after two or three revolutions, disappear. They will resume later, as indicated.*
>
> *At first only centerstage is fully lit up. A rocking-chair stands on porch floor, slightly off to the right from center, upstage. Mrs. Lot, a woman in her fifties, on the heavy side, with soft features, hair too blond for her age and a Mona Lisa smile, rocks gently in chair. She has a paper fan in her hand. She speaks in a dreamy voice.*

Mrs. LOT —When forty years ago we moved to this part of town, it was a quiet neighborhood. Not distinguished, but still . . . respectable. Yes, respectable. A covey of quail lived in the backyard and the boy next door rode a pony. Cute. I mean, the boy. In summertime, on a Saturday afternoon, when the gentlemen in their shirtsleeves had mowed all the lawns with those funny pushrolls they used back then, there would be a sweet odor of hay floating over the whole development. It was like the country. It was . . . boring. Yes, boring.

Then it began to change. The wrong kind of people moving in. The right kind of people moving out. Rezoning. Dingy little groceries. Service stations. Body shops. Warehouses. Truckers. Big, strong, with thighs like oak trees. At least they looked it. Soon our house was the only residence left in the area. With liquor half-pints lying in the gutter on Sunday morning.

Then it changed again. They came. They took over. Now we have a bar where it says "topless", and a bar where it says "bottomless", and a yellow shop with no window and blinking yellow bulbs all around where it says "marital aids", and a cinema where it says "if the show might offend you, do not come in: it is sexplicit." Yes, sexplicit. And, can you imagine, it's right next door, and I've never been. Not that it would offend me. I don't think. But with a husband like your father . . .

The lighted zone has been expanding while Mrs. Lot spoke, so that now we see two other figures: Lola, sitting on steps, and Fernie standing upstage, behind Mrs. Lot and on her right. Lola is blond, with round shoulders, somewhat overweight, her mother's daughter; Fernie is slender, nervous, dark, her father's daughter. Lola slouches, Fernie vibrates; Lola slurs, Fernie spits out, but deep down they are not very different from each other. Both are in late teens.

FERNIE   —Mamma, I need something at the grocery store. I'm going.

LOLA   —Mamma, I need something at the drugstore. I'm going too.

Mrs. Lot goes on rocking, smiling and fanning herself.

FERNIE   —Mamma, I need to buy some hair remover.

LOLA   —Mamma, I need to get some deodorant.

No answer from Mrs. Lot. No movement from the girls.

LOLA   (*pitiful*)—Mom, I simply have to.

FERNIE   (*angry*)—Mom, I've got to, I look like a shaggy rug.

LOLA   —No one cares how you look, you ape.

FERNIE   —No one cares how you smell, you polecat. Mom! . . .

LOLA   —Mummy dear . . .

In the house, a cuckoo sings six times. Mrs. Lot checks her watch.

Mrs. LOT   —Not after six. You know what your father said.

LOLA   —Oh! Mom!

FERNIE   —After six! After six! What's wrong with after six?

Mrs. LOT —You know what's wrong. Your father says there is nothing they won't do in those streets after six. He always tries to be home by six. He should already be in. He says one day he was late and they nearly raped him. (*Revolving lights, slowly.*)

LOLA —Dad?

FERNIE —They must be desperate.

Mrs. LOT —(*gets up*)—You tell him that. He is a good one to argue with, your father is. Yes, a good one. (*Limps toward door.*) If I was your age . . .

FERNIE —What do you mean?

Mrs. LOT enters house without answering. FERNIE comes and sits beside LOLA. Whiff of music. Then music and revolving lights stop.

FERNIE —Mom is all right.

LOLA —Yeah. D'you think she . . .? (*Indicates downtown.*)

FERNIE —No.

LOLA —No?

FERNIE —But she'd have liked to.

LOLA —It's all Dad then.

FERNIE —You've said it.

LOLA —And d'you think that . . .?

FERNIE —We're here, aren't we?

FERNIE gets up and walks off left.

LOLA —What are we going to do tonight?

FERNIE —As usual. Starve. Thirst. Burn. Jump on the pogo stick. Kiss our pictures in the mirror. (*Wrings her hands and shouts:*) Burn!

LOLA —(*looking toward "downtown"*) Wait. Here is Tom. And Sam.

FERNIE —Much good they will do us.

Nevertheless both girls take attitudes. LOLA runs and lies in rocker. FERNIE perches on balustrade, stage left. TOM and SAM walk in from "downtown". Both blond, both on the fat side, both a little sleepy, TOM more than SAM. SAM chews gum, TOM uses bubble-gum.

FERNIE —Hi.

LOLA   —Hi.

SAM   —Hi.

TOM   —Aw shucks! Do you people have to be that formal?

Boys sit on steps with backs to girls. Silence.

LOLA   —You boys going somewhere?

SAM   —No.

LOLA   —You coming from somewhere?

SAM   —No.

LOLA   —You must be coming from somewhere.

SAM   —Guess so.

LOLA   —Wherefrom?

SAM   —(*indicates "downtown"*)—Down there.

FERNIE   —You've been to a bar?

SAM   —Yep.

FERNIE   —Was it fun?

SAM   (*sadly*)—Yeah. Great fun. I mean, great fun. What you say, Tom?

TOM   —Aw shucks. (*Blows a bubble.*)

FERNIE   —Any girls around?

SAM   —Plenty.

FERNIE   —Were they cute?

SAM   —We couldn't see.

FERNIE   —Why not?

SAM   —They didn't have a stitch on.

FERNIE   —Sam, come here.

SAM reluctantly gets up and walks to her. She is still sitting on balustrade. He stays on ground level and leans against balustrade.

FERNIE   —Sam, will you marry me? (*No answer. She puts her hands on his shoulders. He cringes.*) Sam, will you take me somewhere with you? (*He gets toothpick out and cleans teeth.*) Sam, will you take me, period?

SAM   —What's the hurry?

FERNIE recovers hands, closes eyes, on verge of breakdown. SAM, relieved, goes on cleaning teeth.

LOLA   —Tom? (*No answer. She gets up and stands by rocker.*) Tom?!

TOM   (*uncomfortable*)—Tom, Tom. I know I'm Tom. So what?

LOLA   —Come here.

TOM   —Aw shucks.

Tom goes up steps, stands out of reach of LOLA. At least he thinks so. She playfully pushes him into rocker, leans over him, crowds him.

LOLA   —Tom, Dad does not allow us to go out after six. But don't you want to come and see the attic with me? All my stuffed animals are there. Don't you want me to show them to you? There is a pink donkey with flapping ears, and a green snake, and a yellow elephant with a long, long trunk. Don't you want to see them, Tom? In the attic?

TOM   (*blows a bubble*)—I've got a better idea. Why don't we all pile up in a car and go to the drive-in?

LOLA   (*angry*)—What's the use of going to the drive-in with you? All you do is look at the movie. Get out of my way, you . . . you . . . you impotent!

She pretends to walk very fast to the door. There she stops, still expecting some repartee. TOM scratches his head and looks for one.

TOM   (*finally*)—Well, it's a sexy movie.

FERNIE walks up to LOLA.

FERNIE   —Lola?

LOLA   —Fernie?

FERNIE   —What's wrong with those boys?

LOLA   —I dunno. Must be sick or something.

SAM   —We're sick all right. We're sick of your chasing us. I was no more 'n thirteen when Betsie Zeller she put some ants in my jeans so I'd have to take them off. Let's go to my place, Tom, and watch TV. Good clean triple X stuff on the Adults-only station.

TOM   —Fine by me. (*No hard feelings*) Nice seeing you, girls.

SAM   (*None either*)—See you tomorrow, girls. Might have a little chat or something.

TOM and SAM hurry out toward downtown. Music resumes very low. Lights begin to revolve again, a little faster this time.

262

FERNIE crosses LOLA and goes and stands over balustrade on right.

FERNIE   (*looking toward "downtown"*)—Lola.

LOLA   —Fernie?

FERNIE extends left arm, as if groping for LOLA's hand. LOLA walks up to her and gives it to her.

LOLA   —What?

FERNIE   —Let's go.

LOLA   —Where?

FERNIE   —There.

LOLA   —What will Dad say?

FERNIE   —Who cares? He will be stoned. He won't notice. And if he does . . . We have to live our lives, Lola. The way everyone else does. Not the way everyone did in his time, before they came. Do you realize we are virgins? The shame of it!

LOLA   —Well, more or less.

FERNIE   —And there is no counting on those boys, right?

LOLA   —Yes, but there, you know what they'll do to you?

FERNIE   —They'll make me one of them. Don't you want to be one of them? Come on!

For no reason, they climb over the balustrade, drop to "the street" and run in the direction of "downtown". Mr. LOT enters from "the country". He is dark, small in build, but very strong. The music has been growing while the girls were climbing, but his voice covers it easily, and, with his speech, the revolving lights stop.

Mr. LOT   —Hey! Where do you think you're going?

They stop.

Mr. LOT   —Fernie! Lola! I'm talking to you.

They turn toward him. He stares at them, forcing them to come to him where he stands, at the foot of the steps. FERNIE comes first. When she is near enough, he slaps her face, and at the sound of the slap the music stops.

Mr. LOT   —Slut!

FERNIE   (*swallowing her tears, but not without admiration for his manliness*)—Thank you, sir.

Mr. LOT   —Go inside. Help your mother cook supper.

She goes up the steps. When LOLA comes near, Mr. Lot makes a threatening gesture with back of hand. She cowers away after FERNIE. FERNIE walks straight into house, but LOLA pauses a second on the threshold to throw a strange glance at her father. When the girls have left, Mr. LOT walks slowly up the steps and to the rocker, where he sits. Takes a hip flask from pocket and sips. Lights change as sunset moves on. The sun is setting in "the country", and its rays are horizontal and reddish. A long silence, with just a police siren and then a dog barking far away.

Two men, preceded by long shadows, come in from "the country". They are tall, lean, very pale, with broad shoulders and a slight expression of surprise (makeup) never leaving their faces. They look as if they were thirty at the most, but their hair is pure silver. They are dressed like hikers, with boots, light khaki clothes and big, extra-big, rucksacks. They look as much alike as possible, but KEZEF is slightly less tall and strong than AF. They both speak differently from the other characters; whatever they say must sound as if it had another meaning than the obvious one. They look around, but they do not notice Mr. LOT who is lighting a pipe in his rocker.

KEZEF   —Here?

AF   —Here.

They take their backpacks off, with some difficulty, especially KEZEF.

AF   —Heavy, eh?

KEZEF   —The heaviest thing in the world.

They sit down on the ground, at right of steps, leaning tiredly against lower part of porch.

KEZEF   —Is it as you expected it?

AF   —It's worse than Gomorrah. Poor beggars!

KEZEF   —They know they are miserable, but they don't know why.

AF   —They have to be stopped before they destroy themselves completely.

KEZEF   —Why are they doing that to one another?

AF   —And to themselves!

KEZEF   —They hate one another.

AF   —They hate themselves.

KEZEF   —And they call it love.

AF   —It is unlove. What was given them to multiply they use to divide.

KEZEF   —What was given them to differentiate they use to squash.

AF   —Whenever you go too far in one direction, you find yourself at the other end of the world.

KEZEF   —Because the world is round.

AF   —The world is round. (*Revolving lights, twice.*) And it has cancer. (*Looking around*) And this is the tumor.

KEZEF   (*taps rucksack*)—And that is the cure.

AF   —Let's get the sleeping bags out.

They begin to do so. Unobserved, Mr. LOT has come to lean on the balustrade above their heads.

Mr. LOT —Hello, boys.

They are not startled. They lift their heads slowly, but he has to have his little joke. He takes his pipe out of his mouth.

Mr. LOT —Startled you, did I? What d'you think you're doing, anyway?

AF   —We shall spend the night here. (*Goes on with preparations.*)

KEZEF   —We won't be in your way.

Mr. LOT —You can't sleep here.

KEZEF   —It isn't cold, sir.

Mr. LOT —You'll find it hotter a little later.

KEZEF   —We don't mind the heat.

Mr. LOT —I think you would, my boy, the kind of heat I'm talking about. You don't look to me as if you were one of them. Neither of you. You must have hiked some distance!

KEZEF   —We did.

Mr. LOT —Kind of foreign you two boys look to me.

AF   —We are.

Mr. LOT —Well, I wouldn't allow two poor stupid foreigners to get in trouble under my windows.

KEZEF —In trouble, sir?

Mr. LOT —After sundown, there is no law any more in this part of town. Police move out. Cannot contain them any more after sundown. They are pretty brazen in the daytime, but at night . . . (*Whistles*.) And they are so fed up with one another, whenever fresh meat arrives, they tear it to pieces.

KEZEF —You mean the men?

Mr. LOT —The men, the women, how do I know? They don't know themselves any more. There was a couple, the other day: newly-weds, white streamers on the car, "Now it's legal", all that stuff. Thought it would be fun to come and spend their honeymoon. Go to the experts, the sexperts they call themselves. Learn a few tricks.

AF —Well?

Mr. LOT —Two days later, the police found them in the hotel dumpster. (*Puffs on pipe*.) So you're not spending the night outside. You can sleep in the living room. And if you need to wash up, the plumbing is working.

He turns his back on them and walks toward house. They pick up their heavy rucksacks and follow him on porch. Still walking, Mr. LOT prepares to take a sip from his flask, then remembers his manners, and half-turning to KEZEF on his left, offers the flask.

Mr. LOT —Care for a sip, son?

KEZEF —No, sir. Thank you.

Mr. LOT (*turning to AF*)—What about you?

AF —Thank you, no.

Mr. LOT —I thought so.

He takes a gulp himself and is about to enter house, when AF puts down his rucksack and says:

AF —Mr. Lot?

Mr. LOT pivots slowly toward him.

Mr. LOT —How do you know my name?

Brief pause of embarrassment. KEZEF saves situation by setting his rucksack down and advancing with outstretched hand:

KEZEF —I am Kezef. Glad to know you, sir.

Mr. LOT turns and shakes his hand.

AF —I am Af.

Mr. LOT shakes his hand.

Mr. LOT —That sounds . . . Hungarian, doesn't it?

AF —Not exactly.

Mr. LOT —Do they all have that kind of name where you come from?

KEZEF —No. There is one named Mike. That's simple enough.

Mr. LOT —Buddy of yours?

AF —A senior executive in our firm. Mr. Lot, we want to thank you for taking us in.

KEZEF (*looking at AF over Mr. LOT*)—So intelligence was wrong?

AF —Yes, there is one righteous man in the city.

Mr. LOT (*deeply surprised*)—Who's that?

AF —You.

Mr. LOT —Me? Righteous? You must be kidding. (*Chuckles.*) You go and tell the wife that. (*Seriously*) No, sir, I'm not righteous. (*Shows flask.*) I'm an old drunkard. I'm a sot. I'm a brawler. I'm a wife-beater. (*Mysteriously*) I've been known to steal wood from the plant to repair my fence. No way, sir, I could be righteous.

KEZEF —At least you are not like them.

Mr. LOT walks down right. Revolving lights strike him. He takes a meditative sip, the first one to make him slightly drunk. He turns toward visitors.

Mr. LOT —I'm worse, boys. Much worse. When I'm sober, at least I try to keep my house clean. But when I've had a couple too many, lately especially . . . strange thoughts have been crawling into my head. Even in my family, boys, even in my family, God only knows what I might not do.

AF (*softly*)—He does.

KEZEF   —Still, you've decided to protect us.

Mr. LOT   —That's because you're foreigners. Who would want a retarded child to get hurt? Same thing. I'll go and tell the wife to fry some more chicken. (*Tries to pick up visitors' rucksacks. Cannot.*) My, they're heavy.

AF   —They are. Leave them here, please.

Mr. LOT   —Glad to. Don't think I could lift them if I tried.

> *Mr. LOT enters house. KEZEF, crossing AF, walks down to left balustrade, peers into "downtown" area, and sighs. AF, crossing behind him, does the same thing and stands even closer to balustrade. They exchange a meanful look, where one reads both pity and resolution. AF turns away toward right and stands wrapped in a dream. FERNIE enters from house on tiptoe, observes visitors, trying to pick the likelier one. Then she comes down to KEZEF.*

FERNIE   (*low*)—Mister?

KEZEF   —Good evening.

FERNIE   —Hi. Dad says you've hiked a long way.

KEZEF   —We have.

FERNIE   —Whereabouts do you come from?

> *KEZEF shrugs very slightly. FERNIE takes him by the hand and pulls him to downstage right.*

FERNIE   —Tell me, are the girls any good where you come from?

KEZEF   (*seriously*)—They are very good girls.

FERNIE   (*not knowing if she was misunderstood*)—Are they cute?

KEZEF   —They are very beautiful.

FERNIE   (*grasps his arm*)—Am I beautiful?

KEZEF   —You could be.

FERNIE   (*lets go*)—You mean if I shaved my legs.

KEZEF   —I do not mean that.

FERNIE   —What do you mean?

KEZEF   —If you let the light shine through you.

> *FERNIE makes a grimace: she is puzzled. She looks away from KEZEF who beams at her with tenderness. Enter LOLA. She walks up to AF.*

LOLA   —Hey.

AF   —Hey.

LOLA   —You spending the night with us?

No answer. She notices his hair.

LOLA   —How come you've got white hair when you're so young? Not that I mind. In fact, I think it's lovely, you know. Exotic. Kind of (*giggles*) gives you the creeps. I like to have the creeps. Honest. I like you. D'you like me?

AF   (*seriously*)—I love you.

LOLA   —Wow! So sudden! What are you going to do about it?

AF   —You'll see.

LOLA   —You don't have to tell lies. I'm not asking for love. Not for real love, I mean.

AF   —Why don't you? That's what you deserve.

Lets her stand, amazed. Crosses over to KEZEF.

Mr. LOT   (*appears in doorway*)—So, d'you want the fried chicken or don't you (*Suddenly he freezes, pointing toward "downtown".*) Here they come!

Lights dimmed. Revolving lights on, full speed. Music on, full blast. THEY enter from "downtown". Not less than 5, not more than 13 characters, dressed up as acid colored stuffed animals. One recognizes donkeys, elephants, snakes and others. Impossible to know men from women. They dance a frenzied dance, uttering groans, moans, growls, roars, hisses, but at no time one human sound. This should be both grotesque and nightmarish.

LOLA and FERNIE have jumped back closer to their father. Mrs. LOT appears from behind him and watches the proceedings, fascinated, with her Mona Lisa smile. AF and KEZEF stand, looking at the frantic ballet in "the street". When they turn their heads to exchange a glance, the dancers notice them. Surprise. Interest. Desire. Some go on dancing, others exchange impressions. Mewings and lowings of appreciation. Calls, gestures, both engaging and vaguely ferocious, meaning "Come down here, we like you." AF and KEZEF do not move. The light falls so that their faces cannot be seen.

Mr. LOT   —Leave them alone! Get out of here! They are not your kind.

269

More seductive dancing. No reaction from AF and KEZEF. Threats follow. Some dancers crawl up steps, stretching out greedy hands.

Mr. LOT —Leave them alone, I say. You two, get into the house. We'll lock the door.

Mrs. LOT —They'd better not. I don't want my doors and windows broken.

Mr. LOT —There are enough of you to have fun together. Don't touch my foreigners. Don't touch my guests.

Mrs. LOT —Your guests are going to be the death of your family.

FERNIE and LOLA cling to their father. The dancers climb on the balustrade. They are going to lay hands on AF and KEZEF. Music expresses utter possession. Mr. LOT takes a long sip from flask, seizes daughters by hair and moves downstage, pushing and pulling them.

Mr. LOT —Hey, you, listen to me. I've got these two here. Not worth much. I've known prettier ones, and some smarter ones, and many better ones. But they are my girls. My two babies. I wanted to keep them from your filthy hands. But they are your kind. Take them, and leave my foreigners alone!

He shoves the girls forward. They fall to their knees. The dancers are wrapped around the columns, spread out on the steps, perched on balustrade. AF awakes from trance, turns toward invaders and slowly raises his hand. We have not seen his palm yet: it is the color of silver and it glows in the dark. Music stops. Revolving lights go on. Dancers utter animal shrieks of pain and cover their eyes with their paws. They have been blinded. FERNIE and LOLA creep up to see what AF holds in his hand: they think it is some weapon.

KEZEF —Don't look! Don't look!

Girls stop. Dancers rock to and fro and moan. For the first time something slightly human seems to come from them: it sounds like "It hurts . . ."

AF *(hand still lifted, still looking at dancers)*—Mr. Lot?

Mr. LOT (*has remembered his military days*)—Sir?

AF —In a few minutes, life will have ceased in this city. You, because there is still some hope of recovery for you, will be spared. Is there anyone whom you want to take with you?

Mr. LOT —Guess I have to take the wife.

AF —Anyone else?

Mr. LOT —My girls, that's for sure.

FERNIE —I'd like to take Sam.

LOLA —I'd like to take Tom.

KEZEF —Take them. (*Both girls get up.*)

LOLA (*shouts*)—Tom! Where are you, Tom, you no-gooder, you?

FERNIE (*shouts*)—Sam? Where are you, Sam, you lazy oaf?

SAM (*in the back of the audience*)—We're not coming.

TOM (*in the back of the audience*)—We're watching TV It's good!

FERNIE —You're going to die!

SAM —You're a smart kid, Fernie. You aren't going to believe those two jokers.

LOLA —You're going to die. Then what?

TOM —Aw, shucks!

SAM —We're going to die, but they've never lived!

KEZEF lifts silver palm. TOM and SAM shriek and cover eyes with forearms.

AF —Kezef, their time has run out.

KEZEF walks to rucksacks, kneels to open them.

Mr. LOT —What's in those heavy bags?

AF (*slowly lowers his hand*)—The wrath of God.

KEZEF —The compassion of God.

AF —It is the same thing.

KEZEF opens one rucksack. Audience and actors see it is empty.

Mrs. LOT —There's nothing in that one.

Mr. LOT —How come they were so . . . (*indicates heaviness*)?

AF   —I told you. Now depart and do not look back. No man shall see the compassion of God and live.

KEZEF prepares to open second rucksack. Blackout. The moans cease one by one. Silence. When lights with a greenish tint flood stage, the dancers all lie dead in different postures. AF and KEZEF have disappeared. The LOT family is huddled together on "street" level, stage left, facing "country".

Mrs. LOT —I'll take a peep . . . Yes, a peep.

She turns back, takes a step toward dancers, stands petrified, with mouth open. Something floats down from ceiling.

FERNIE   —Lola?

LOLA   —Fernie?

FERNIE   *(catches it)*—What is it?

LOLA   —A feather. I wonder where it comes from.

The two girls look at each other, puzzled. Lights go slowly out.